ADVANCES

A Univocal Book

Drew Burk, Consulting Editor

Univocal Publishing was founded by Jason Wagner and Drew Burk as an independent publishing house specializing in artisanal editions and translations of texts spanning the areas of cultural theory, media archaeology, continental philosophy, aesthetics, and anthropology. In 2017 Univocal ceased operations as a publisher and became a series with its publishing partner, the University of Minnesota Press.

Univocal authors include:

Miguel Abensour
Judith Balso
Jean Baudrillard
Philippe Beck
Simon Critchley
Fernand Deligny
Jacques Derrida
Vinciane Despret
Georges Didi-Huberman
Jean Epstein
Vilém Flusser
Barbara Glowczewski
Evelyne Grossman
Félix Guattari
David Lapoujade
François Laruelle

David Link
Sylvère Lotringer
Jean Malaurie
Michael Marder
Quentin Meillassoux
Friedrich Nietzsche
Peter Pál Pelbart
Jacques Rancière
Lionel Ruffel
Michel Serres
Gilbert Simondon
Étienne Souriau
Isabelle Stengers
Eugene Thacker
Siegfried Zielinski

Jacques Derrida

ADVANCES

Translated and with an Introduction by
Philippe Lynes

A Univocal Book

University of Minnesota Press
Minneapolis
London

The University of Minnesota Press acknowledges the contribution of Jason Wagner, Univocal's publisher, in making this volume possible.

Originally published in French as "Avances," in Serge Margel, *Le Tombeau du dieu artisan,* in 1995; copyright 1995 by Les Éditions de Minuit.

Published by the University of Minnesota Press
111 Third Avenue South, Suite 290
Minneapolis, MN 55401-2520
http://www.upress.umn.edu

Printed in the United States of America on acid-free paper

The University of Minnesota is an equal-opportunity educator and employer.

22 21 20 19 18 17   10 9 8 7 6 5 4 3 2 1

Library of Congress Cataloging-in-Publication Data
Names: Derrida, Jacques, author.
Title: Advances / Jacques Derrida ; translated and with an introduction by Philippe Lynes.
Other titles: Avances. English
Description: Minneapolis : University of Minnesota Press, 2017. | Series: Univocal | "A Univocal book." |
Identifiers: LCCN 2017051219 | ISBN 978-1-5179-0426-5 (pb)
Subjects: LCSH: Margel, Serge. Tombeau du Dieu artisan. | Plato. Timaeus. | Cosmology, Ancient.
Classification: LCC B387.M373 D4713 2018 | DDC 194—dc23
LC record available at https://lccn.loc.gov/2017051219

Socrates. And that is to put oneself in the most natural way in the very place of the God. Now, of all acts the most complete is that of constructing. . . . The Demiurge was pursuing his own designs, which do not concern his creatures. The converse of this must come to pass. . . . But I come after him. . . .

Phaedrus. It is fortunate for them that you are a dead architect! . . . But do you mean to revoke in eternity all those sayings that made you immortal?

Socrates. Immortal there—relatively to mortals! . . . —But here . . . But . . . there is no here, and all that we have been saying is as much a natural sport of the silence of these nether regions as the fantasy of some rhetorician of the other world who has used us as puppets!

Phaedrus. It is in this that immortality rigorously consists.

— Paul Valéry, *Eupalinos, or The Architect* (*in fine*)

Contents

Introduction

Auparadvances

Philippe Lynes

> What is it again one calls a preface? I would ask. Answer: well, that from which this book frees itself *in advance,* better than so many others. It must do so and does so. It emancipates itself from the authority alleged by this law of genre—as if by everything it presupposes. Truthfully, in excessively extending this notion of a "preface," I would be tempted to see in this book a relentless "return inquiry" to everything that comes *before* it . . . even "philosophy" itself.
>
> —Jacques Derrida, "La Forme et la façon"[1]

–1. "Before Even the '*Fore-word*'"

What if, playing a little with a famous remark of Whitehead's,[2] one were to read the history of philosophy as

---

1 Jacques Derrida, "La Forme et la façon (plus jamais: envers et contre tout, ne plus jamais penser ça 'pour la forme,'" in Alain David, *Racisme et antisémitisme: Essai de philosophie sur l'envers de concepts* (Paris: Ellipses, 2001), 8–9; emphasis modified. Where no published translation of a given work by Derrida exists, the one cited will be our own.

2 "The safest general characterization of the European philosophical tradition is that it consists of a series of footnotes to

fore-words to Plato—not in some pre-Socratic sense, although the ambiguity one might hear in the German *Vorsokratiker,* where the *vor* lends itself to the same temporal and spatial difficulties as the English "before," already gives way to what could exceed the economies and chronologies of philosophical debt and restitution, or the traffic of inheritances at play in the familial dramaturgies of *The Post Card: From Socrates to Freud and Beyond.* Not only with respect to how philosophy stands *before* Platonism, *owes* itself to Platonism, and must repay its advances, but also as it tries to get ahead of it [*le devancer*]*,* to take the lead [*prendre de l'avance*] at times in the same movement as it reimagines what precedes it or comes before [*avant*] it, in the case before [*devant*] us, what precedes being and time themselves.[3]

Plato" (Alfred North Whitehead, *Process and Reality: An Essay in Cosmology* [London: Free Press, 1978], 39). For this section's title, see Jacques Derrida, *Moscou aller-retour, Suivi d'un entretien avec N. Avtonomova, V. Podoroga, M. Ryklin* (La Tour d'Aigues: Éditions de l'Aube, 1995), 63.

3   "Before" in English of course refers both to temporal anteriority, the sense of the French *avant,* and the spatial position of standing "before," in front or ahead of something heard in the French *devant.* "Before," however, does not capture *devant* as the present participle of the verb *devoir,* expressing duty, necessity, or obligation. Derrida has, of course, played on these equivocations in "Before the Law" in *Acts of Literature,* ed. Derek Attridge, trans. Avital Ronell and Christine Roulson (London: Routledge, 1992).

Derrida recalls in *The Post Card* that the traditional philosophical lineage tells us that "Socrates comes *before* [*avant*] Plato, there is between them—and in general—an order of generations, an

Introduction

Derrida's 1995 foreword to Serge Margel's *Le Tombeau du dieu artisan* is here published for the first time in English translation, and, despite serving as a frequent point of reference in Derrida's own work, re-

---

irreversible sequence of inheritance. Socrates is before [*avant*], not in front of [*devant*] but before [*avant*] Plato, therefore behind him, and the charter binds us to this order: this is how to orient one's thought, this is the left and this is the right, march" (Jacques Derrida, *The Post Card: From Socrates to Freud and Beyond,* trans. Alan Bass [Chicago: University of Chicago Press, 1987], 20; translation modified). Describing the famous postcard where Socrates is seen writing *before* [*devant*] Plato as nothing less than an apocalyptic revelation, where one does not know who is before [*devant*] or behind the other, the postcard "allegorizes the catastrophic unknown of the order. Finally, one begins no longer to understand what to come [*venir*], to come before, to come after, to foresee [*prévenir*], to come back [*revenir*] all mean—along with the difference of the generations, and then to inherit, to write one's will, to dictate, to speak, to take dictation, etc. We are finally going to be able to love ourselves or one another [*s'aimer*]. All of this is not without, it is not to all of you that I will have to teach this, political consequences. They are still difficult to calculate" (ibid., 21; translation modified). Perhaps everything one could say on Derrida's *Advances* has now already been said.

"Auparadvances," a play on the French *auparavant* (beforehand, anteriorly) and, of course, *avances,* lets us hear the same "*par*" as that complicating any notion of origin in Derrida's reading of Ponge's "Fable": "*Par le mot par commence donc ce texte*" "*Through the word through begins then this text,*" a reading that leads Derrida to the very definition of deconstruction as an experience of the impossible. Cf. Jacques Derrida, "Psyche: Invention of the Other," in *Psyche: Inventions of the Other, Volume I,* ed. Peggy Kamuf and Elizabeth Rottenberg, trans. Catherine Porter (Stanford, Calif.: Stanford University Press, 2007). Timaeus's own "fable"

mains rarely studied in English-speaking deconstructive scholarship.[4] *Advances,* however, is presented here as if disjointed, expropriated, cut off from its source or *oikos*—just like the "enigmatic preamble to a preface"[5] cited here in epigraph—in a violence perhaps not dissimilar from breaking into a familial tomb or *oikesis,* reinterring the bodies apart from one another and engraving new inscriptions upon each stele. As this fore-

---

of the Demiurge will likewise give us to think "the beginning in the beginning, the beginning before or after the beginning (πάλιν ἀρκτέον ἀπ᾽ ἀρχῆς, says the *Timaeus*)." Cf. "The Countertime of Philosophy," *Advances.*

4   For references to *Advances* in Derrida's other work, see *Monolingualism of the Other or The Prosthesis of Origin,* trans. Patrick Mensah (Stanford, Calif.: Stanford University Press, 1998), 77n3, 93n11; *Adieu to Emmanuel Levinas,* trans. Pascale-Anne Brault and Michael Naas (Stanford, Calif.: Stanford University Press, 1999), 147n93; "Faith and Knowledge: Two Sources of 'Religion' at the Limits of Reason Alone," in *Acts of Religion,* ed. Gil Anidjar, trans. Samuel Weber (New York: Routledge, 2002), 94n38; *On Touching—Jean-Luc Nancy,* trans. Christine Irizzary (Stanford, Calif.: Stanford University Press, 2005), 331n24; "As If It Were Possible, 'Within Such Limits,'" in *Paper Machine,* trans. Rachel Bowlby (Stanford, Calif.: Stanford University Press, 2005), 196n28; "Typewriter Ribbon: Limited Ink (2)," in *Without Alibi,* ed. and trans. Peggy Kamuf (Stanford, Calif.: Stanford University Press, 2002), 297n35; "Marx & Sons," in *Ghostly Demarcations: A Symposium on Jacques Derrida's "Spectres of Marx,"* ed. Michael Sprinker, trans. G. M. Goshgarian (London: Verso, 2008), 224; "Questions à Jacques Derrida," in *La Philosophie au risque de la promesse,* ed. Marc Crépon and Marc de Launay (Paris: Bayard, 2004), 202.

5   Derrida, "La Forme et la façon," 8.

word is being inscribed, the demiurgic inventor of the tomb that is Serge Margel prepares his own new foreword to an English edition of *The Tomb of the Artisan God,* to be published with the University of Minnesota Press,[6] his book thereby emancipated (although it, too, was so in advance) from Derrida's *Advances,* letting the promise of both texts be heard anew and otherwise, each having been given a new space to breathe through this ex-appropriation.

What *Advances* promises is nothing less than a non-metaphysical concept of time, the *"autre temps"* mentioned in "Tense," the disjointure of time the *exordium* in *Spectres of Marx* announces as the very condition of justice, and an entire reorganization of the space of the ethico-politico-juridical, the ecological, and of what it means to dwell on the space of the earth.[7] This

---

6   Serge Margel, *Le Tombeau du dieu artisan: Sur Platon* (Paris: Éditions de Minuit, 1995); English edition, *The Tomb of the Artisan God: On Plato's Timaeus,* trans. Philippe Lynes (Minneapolis: University of Minnesota Press, forthcoming).

7   Jacques Derrida, "Tense," in *The Path of Archaic Thinking: Unfolding the Work of John Sallis,* ed. Kenneth Maly, trans. David Farrell Krell (Albany: State University of New York Press, 1995), 49; Jacques Derrida, *Spectres of Marx,* trans. Peggy Kamuf (London: Routledge Classics, 2006), xviii–xx. The discussions between John Sallis and Derrida on *khōra* are themselves a fascinating site for further investigation on the subject of time. See especially Sallis, *Chorology: On Beginning in Plato's "Timaeus"* (Bloomington: Indiana University Press, 1999); "De la Chora," in *Le Passage des frontières* (Paris: Galilée, 1994); and "Of the Χώρα," *Epoché* 2 (1994): 1–12. See also "As If It Were Possible," 93.

time cannot be thought or known in philosophy; its promise as irreducible to speech-act theory as its gift to phenomenological givenness in intuition; it can only be imagined or dreamt, and this dream is precisely the invention of the other that the "fabulous *récit*" of the *Timaeus* will have given us; the time of an aneconomic, irreversible, and originary expenditure that is also the condition of the absolute, an-archic gift, that is, the impossible—the time philosophy will have always attempted to counter and restitute through "the powerful concept of the *possible* that runs through Western thought, from Aristotle to Kant and Husserl (then differently to Heidegger) . . . but also power, capacity, everything that renders skilled, or able, or that formally enables, and so on."[8]

Derrida had, of course, long understood the aneconomic as a movement of différance; "relation to an impossible presence, as expenditure without reserve, as the irreparable loss of presence, the irreversible usage of energy, that is, as the death drive, and as the relation to the wholly other that apparently interrupts every economy."[9] We can better understand

---

8   Derrida, "As If It Were Possible," 90. For more on the gift as the impossible and aneconomic, see Jacques Derrida, *Given Time: 1. Counterfeit Money,* trans. Peggy Kamuf (Chicago: University of Chicago Press, 1994), 5–7.

9   Jacques Derrida, "Différance," in *Margins of Philosophy,* trans. Alan Bass (Brighton: Harvester Press, 1982), 19; translation modified. For Derrida's reading of the aneconomic in Bataille's general economy, see "From Restricted to General Economy: A Hegelian-

the significance of the Demiurge's own death drive or symbolic death, its powerlessness and inoperativity through Derrida's reflections on the limits and paradoxes of the possible as economy, power, or propriety in *The Post Card,* where he relates the notion of time in Freud's death drive with "the auto-affective structure of time (that which there gives itself to receive is no present-being) such as it is described in Husserl's *Lectures on Internal Time Consciousness* or Heidegger's *Kantbuch,*" mentioning in a footnote the intention to develop this in *Given Time.*[10] While Derrida claims elsewhere that matters in the latter seminar have "expressly oriented all the texts I have published since about 1972"[11]–particularly

---

ism without Reserve," in *Writing and Difference,* trans. Alan Bass (London: Routledge Classics, 2001).

10   Derrida, *The Post Card,* 359 and note 6. The material published in the book *Given Time,* however, does not develop this claim, as it only constitutes the first five sessions of a seminar of the same name given in 1977–78 at the École Normale Supérieure, in 1978–79 at Yale, and again more than a decade later in April 1991 at the University of Chicago. Cf. *Séminaire: Donner le temps,* Jacques Derrida Papers, University of California at Irvine Critical Theory Archives, MS-C01, Box 14, Folders 9–12. In *Parages,* moreover, Derrida expresses a desire to publish together the seminar notes for *Donner le temps,* the three years of *La Chose* on Ponge (1975), Blanchot (1976), and Freud (1978), and two other seminars on Blanchot, *Du Droit à la littérature* (1978) and *Thomas l'obscur* (1979). Cf. Jacques Derrida, *Parages,* trans. Tom Conley et al. (Stanford, Calif.: Stanford University Press, 2011), 5.

11   Jacques Derrida, "How to Avoid Speaking: Denials," in *Psyche: Inventions of the Other, Volume II,* ed. Peggy Kamuf and Eliz-

Heidegger's "es gibt" of time and space anterior to being—he also develops an extensive bibliography in its published sections detailing the germinations of this thought in his earliest work.[12] Perhaps the most striking of these, for our purposes, is the discussion in his 1964 "Violence and Metaphysics" relating Levinas's "il y a" to the "es gibt" and on the question of "the gift of the world to the other as wholly other . . . the gift of the world to the other who is *above Being*."[13]

That the promise or the gift of the world or the earth would be "older" than the time of Kantian transcendental philosophy, Husserlian phenomenology, or Heideggerian ontology is one of the most provocative claims in *Advances*. It is through dreaming or imagining our relation *without* relation to this otherwise than being of time, akin to Levinas's past that has never been present[14] or Blanchot's "'terrifyingly ancient' time,"[15] that the auto-affective time of philosophy finds itself both comprised and exceeded by the wholly other, in an "advance without advance [in which] the *without* auto-affects itself by the wholly other (*without without*

abeth Rottenberg, trans. Ken Frieden and Elizabeth Rottenberg (Stanford, Calif.: Stanford University Press, 2008), 313n24.

12 Derrida, *Given Time,* ix.

13 Jacques Derrida, "Violence and Metaphysics: An Essay on the Thought of Emmanuel Levinas," in *Writing and Difference,* 185; translation modified.

14 Cf. Jacques Derrida, *Of Grammatology,* trans. Gayatri Chakravorty Spivak (Baltimore: Johns Hopkins University Press, 1974), 70; Derrida, "Différance," 21.

15 Cf. Derrida, *Parages,* 60–61.

without . . .)," as Derrida puts it in "Pas."[16] It is in this "without," moreover, that Derrida will locate the promise of a messianism without messianism, a "without" that, beyond any negativity or annihilation, will give us to hear otherwise the notion of *"terre promise,"* not as "Promised Land" but "promised earth": the promise of a *terre sans terre* following the groundless ground [*fond sans fond*] of *khōra.*[17] *Advances* will thus importantly

---

16   Jacques Derrida, "Pace Not(s)," in *Parages,* trans. John P. Leavey Jr., 79; translation modified.

17   It would be necessary to further illustrate how the notion of *terre sans terre* would exceed that of a Promised Land and its ties to any messianic or eschatological revelation or geographic rootedness. Cf. Derrida, "Faith and Knowledge," 48. See also *Adieu to Emmanuel Levinas,* where Derrida refers to Levinas's "necessary distinction between sacredness and holiness, that is, the holiness of the other, the holiness of the person, who is, as Emmanuel Levinas said elsewhere, 'more holy than a land [*terre*], even when that land is a Holy Land [*Terre Sainte*]. Next to a person who has been affronted, this land [*terre*]—holy and promised—is but nakedness and desert, a heap of wood and stone" (4). It would, of course, also be important to complicate Levinas's humanism on this subject, as Derrida's finite promise of the earth invites us to do.

"Terre sans terre" [*earth without earth*] in French would be homophonous with "terre s'enterre" [*the earth buries or inters itself*]. Such a notion lets us read not only Derrida's own description of the *Timaeus* as a tomb sinking into the earth under the weight of the scholarly imprintings on its subject, but also the notion of *khōra* as a nonmemory, something that must let everything become erased in order to receive the Demiurge's imprints. As Derrida adds in *Advances, khōra* does not even forget, presumably at least insofar as the opposition of memory and forgetting still belongs to the history of metaphysics (cf. *Advances*). This question intersects importantly

contribute not only to Derridean scholarship, particularly regarding Greek philosophy and time, but also to current debates in new materialism, speculative realism, and biopolitical thought, as well as the emerging field of eco-deconstruction.[18]

with the necessity of an absolute or radical forgetting as the an-economic condition of the gift that, Derrida writes in *Given Time*, "should accord with a certain experience of the *trace* as *cinder* or *ashes*" (Derrida, *Given Time*, 17). Derrida then refers in a footnote to the correspondence of the "il y a là" (there is there) with the giving of the gift in *Cinders*, trans. Ned Lukacher (Minneapolis: University of Minnesota Press, 2014), 55. It is further instructive that Derrida uses the syntagm "il y a là" both with reference to *khōra* (cf. Derrida, "How to Avoid Speaking," 172) and with reference to the Demiurge in *Advances*. Just as importantly, the "sans" in the notion of "terre sans terre" would force us to rethink the *oikos* of ecological relationality and life on earth beyond any holism, biocentrism, or symbiosis, and rather in terms of interruption, disjunction, and difference, along the same logic through which Blanchot and Levinas refer to the "relation without relation."

18   For more on Derrida's philosophy of time, see David Wood, *The Deconstruction of Time* (Evanston, Ill.: Northwestern University Press, 2001) and *Time after Time* (Bloomington: Indiana University Press, 2007). See also Martin Hägglund, *Radical Atheism: Derrida and the Time of Life* (Stanford, Calif.: Stanford University Press, 2008), and Joanna Hodge, *Derrida on Time* (London: Routledge, 2007). With respect to new materialism, see especially Derrida's discussion in *Spectres of Marx* concerning "a materialism without substance: a materialism of the *khôra*" (212). Derrida, however, elsewhere cautions against the Aristotelian interpretation of *khōra* as matter (cf. Jacques Derrida, "Khōra," in *On the Name*, ed. Thomas Dutoit, trans. Ian McLeod [Stanford, Calif.: Stanford University Press, 1995], 127, and Derrida, "How to Avoid Speaking," 171).

0—Χώρα: The Pre-Word, or Forewards to Plato

As Derrida famously claims in "Plato's Pharmacy," "we are today on the eve [*veille*] of Platonism."[19] Deconstruction, however, has never meant the simple end, inversion, or reversal of Platonism, but rather, he ex-

---

See also Martin Hägglund's deconstructive critique of Quentin Meillassoux's speculative materialism in "The Arche-Materiality of Time: Deconstruction, Evolution and Speculative Materialism," in *Theory after Theory,* ed. Jane Elliott and Derek Attridge (London: Routledge, 2011), and Peter Gratton's argument in *Speculative Realism: Problems and Prospects* (London: Bloomsbury Academic, 2014) as per Heidegger and Derrida's realism of time against the charge of "correlationism." As concerns the reinterpretations of life and death required in thinking through the biopolitical paradigm, see the discussions of "survivance" in *Advances,* as well as Cary Wolfe's excellent new introduction to *Cinders.* Finally, as concerns eco-deconstruction, or the application of Derrida's philosophy to environmental thought, see especially David Wood, "Spectres of Derrida: On the way to Econstruction," in *Ecospirit: Religions and Philosophies for the Earth,* ed. Laurel Kearns and Catherine Keller (New York: Fordham University Press, 2007), as well as Matthias Fritsch, Philippe Lynes, and David Wood, eds., *Eco-Deconstruction: Derrida and Environmental Philosophy* (New York: Fordham University Press, forthcoming 2018). See especially therein, on the subject of *khōra,* John Llewelyn's "Writing Home: Eco-choro-spectrography," and, concerning *Advances,* our own "The Post-human Promise of the Earth." See also, with respect to Derrida's notion of the gift and environmental thought, Matthias Fritsch's "The Gift of Nature in Mauss and Derrida," *Oxford Literary Review* 37:1(2015): 1–23.

19　Jacques Derrida, "Plato's Pharmacy," in *Dissemination,* trans.

plains in *Monolingualism of the Other,* a certain "hyperbolism" or raising the ante of its stakes:

> Everything that proceeds [*s'avance*] under the name of
> 'deconstruction' arises from it . . . beginning with the 'hyperbole' (it's Plato's word) that will have ordered everything, including the reinterpretation of *khōra,* namely, the passage to the very beyond of the passage of the Good or the One beyond being (*hyperbolē . . . epekeina tēs ousias*), excess beyond excess: impregnable.[20]

Metaphysics will have always itself provided the resources for its own closure and exceeding; this is what

---

Barbara Johnson (London: Athlone Press, 1981), 107. *"Veille"* in French, however, not only lets us hear "eve" but also to keep a vigil, to keep watch, or to stay awake. That the Demiurge's promise occurs in "the time of an eve before time" (cf. "The Countertime of Philosophy, *Advances*) ought be heard in this sense as well. See on this another one of Derrida's prefaces, "The Night Watch (over 'the book of himself')," in *Derrida and Joyce: Texts and Contexts,* ed. Andrew J. Mitchell and Sam Slote, trans. Pascale-Anne Brault and Michael Naas (Albany: State University of New York Press, 2013). On the notion of khōra as "pre-word," see Jacques Derrida and Peter Eisenman, *Chora L Works* (New York: Monacelli Press, 1997), 35: "**PE** So why isn't chora the word? Before God and nature—why not the word? **JD** The word? Because it is not a word. It's pre . . . **PE** Pre-word. **JD** Yes . . . It's only before in the sense of allowing. It's before before."

20 Derrida, *Monolingualism of the Other,* 49. As he continues, the deconstruction of metaphysics will have always consisted of translating its outside into its language, "as if I were still weaving some veil from the wrong side (which many weavers do, I might add), and as if the necessary passage points of this weaving from

fascinates Derrida so much about the *khōra* as introduced in Plato's *Timaeus,* a topic discussed as early as a 1970 seminar.[21] *Khōra* or χώρα in Greek simply means "place," "place in general, the residence, the habitation, the place where we live, the country."[22] In Timaeus's fable of the Demiurge's creation of the sensible world, however, *khōra* for Derrida comes to designate the precise site of resistance to Platonic metaphysics as that which *gives place,* or as *spacing.* It ought already be noted that Timaeus's account belongs to no assured opposition between *logos* or *muthos*; it is rather a "bastard," "impure," or "hybrid" account,

---

the wrong side were places of *transcendence,* of an absolute elsewhere, therefore, in the eyes of Graeco-Latino-Christian Western philosophy, but yet *inside it* (*epekeina tēs ousias,* and beyond—*khōra*—negative theology, Meister Eckhart and beyond, Freud and beyond, a certain Heidegger, Artaud, Levinas, Blanchot, and certain others). . . . the 'elsewhere,' toward which I was myself ex-ported *in advance*" (ibid., 70–71; emphasis modified).

21 Cf. Derrida, "Khōra," 149n7. Derrida refers here to "a seminar held at the École Normale Supérieure in 1970 (Theory of Philosophical Discourse: The Conditions of Inscription of the Text of Political Philosophy—the Example of Materialism)." The Critical Theory Archives at the University of California at Irvine lists a series of two seminars from 1969–70. *Théorie du discours philosophique: la métaphore dans le texte philosophique* (10 sessions) and 1970–71: *Théorie du discours philosophique* (5 sessions): Jacques Derrida Papers, University of California at Irvine Critical Theory Archives, MS-C01, Box 10, Folders 8–17. In both cases, the archive references Derrida's "White Mythology: Metaphor in the Text of Philosophy," in *Margins of Philosophy.*

22 Derrida and Eisenman, *Chora L Works,* 9.

a preorigin to philosophical discourse.[23] *Khōra* must likewise be grasped "as in a dream."[24] In the *Timaeus*, the Demiurge creates the sensible world by fixing his gaze upon the intelligible ideas or paradigms and inscribing their copies upon *khōra*. But *khōra* belongs neither to the eternal world of being nor to the world of becoming; it is neither form nor matter, intelligible nor sensible. It is a third that exceeds and precedes all metaphysical oppositions while making them possible. If Plato designates *khōra* as an imprint-bearer, matrix, mother, nurse, or receptacle, these terms ought not be understood as its metaphors, nor ought they be understood to properly represent *khōra* "as such"; beyond the opposition between metaphor and proper, *khōra* delineates the very impossibility of any "as such."[25] As Derrida explains in both *Faith and Knowledge* and

---

23 "Let us take things up again from farther back, which can be translated thus: let us go back behind and below the assured discourse of philosophy, which proceeds by oppositions of principle and counts on the origin as on a *normal couple*. We must go back toward a preorigin which deprives us of this assurance and requires at the same time an impure philosophical discourse" (Derrida, "Khōra," 125–26). On the subject of bastardry, Derrida also refers to "Plato's Pharmacy" and David Farrell Krell, "Le Plus pur des bâtards," *Revue Philosophique de la France et de l'Étranger* 15:2 (1990): 229–38; cf. "Tense," 284n9.

24 Derrida, "Khōra," 90.

25 On the role of metaphor with respect to *khōra,* see note 21, as well as Derrida, "How to Avoid Speaking," 172, where he also references "The *Retrait* of Metaphor," in *Psyche: Inventions of the Other, Volume I,* trans. Peggy Kamuf.

"How to Avoid Speaking: Denials," *khōra* is beyond any Greco-Abrahamic anthropo-teleological understanding of the *epekeina tēs ousias,* along with the tradition of negative theology that runs back to Plato and Plotinus through to Heidegger and beyond.[26] Its taking-place, whose otherwise than being is neither the Good, God, the Human, nor History would constitute "*the very* site *of an infinite resistance, of an infinitely impassible remaining* [*restance*]."[27] *Khōra* further designates a site without habitation or dwelling, a site *without* site, wholly a-topian or hypertopian, a site of absolute exteriority anterior to the time of creation and time itself, a "before" prior to chronology.[28] It gives place by withdrawing from everything to which it gives place,

---

26   For Derrida's discussion of the *epekeina tēs ousias* and *khōra* with respect to negative theology, see "How to Avoid Speaking," 167–74. For an early discussion of negative theology, see "Différance," 6. In "We Other Greeks," however, Derrida explicitly distinguishes between the two notions insofar as the *epekeina tēs ousias* of the *Republic* or the *Parmenides* still "gives rise to histories, narratives, or myths, and opens a reference to the Good, to God, to some event." *Khōra,* by contrast, would constitute a "non-event." Cf. Jacques Derrida, "We Other Greeks," in *Derrida and Antiquity,* ed. Miriam Leonard, trans. Pascale-Anne Brault and Michael Naas (Oxford: Oxford University Press, 2010), 34–35. Likewise, he adds elsewhere, "it doesn't seem possible to me that the *chora* of the sun in the *Republic* can be a metaphorical value of the *chora* in the *Timaeus*" (Derrida, "As If It Were Possible," 93).

27   Derrida, "Faith and Knowledge," 59. Translation modified. Cf. also "We Other Greeks," 35.

28   Cf. Derrida, *Parages,* 131–32; Derrida, "Faith and Knowledge," 57–58; Jacques Derrida and Jean-Luc Marion, "On the Gift:

as well as from any name that could be ascribed to it. While not nothing, the "thing" that is *khōra* "seems to 'give place'—without, however, this 'thing' ever *giving* anything: neither the ideal paradigms of things nor the copies that an insistent demiurge, the fixed idea before his eyes, inscribes in it."[29] *Khōra* is ultimately "a place of non-gift which makes the gift possible by resisting it."[30]

One of Margel's great insights for Derrida consists in reading the Demiurge as an ultimately mortal being, radically passive, inoperative, and powerless in his incapacity to indefinitely represent the sensible world in the image of the eternal ideas. This architect god will have prepared a dwelling space for mortals having as its condition a pre-originary spacing that expropriates any *oikonomia*.[31] As Derrida points out in *Advances,* Margel's Demiurge is a *surviving* god, a

---

A Discussion between Jacques Derrida and Jean-Luc Marion Moderated by Richard Kearney," in *God, the Gift and Postmodernism,* ed. John D. Caputo and Michael J. Scanlon (Bloomington: Indiana University Press, 1999), 76.

29 Derrida, "Khōra," xv.

30 Derrida and Marion, "On the Gift," 76. Cf. also Derrida, "Questions à Jacques Derrida," 208.

31 The relation between the Demiurge and architecture ought to be developed at length here, especially given Derrida's own choice of epigraph to *Advances* with Valéry's *Eupalinos, or The Architect.* *Khōra* was also to serve as the organizing theme for a collaboration between Derrida and architect Peter Eisenman titled *Chora L Works* based on one of Derrida's drawings of *khōra.* The reader might also consult Derrida's reference to a "transarchitecture" in "No (Point

surviving whose logic clearly ought to be understood in terms of everything Derrida writes about a *survivance* exceeding the opposition of life and death, just as the spacing of *khōra* is neither born nor dies.[32] This structure of survivance is itself the condition of the gift

---

of) Madness—Maintaining Architecture," in *Psyche: Inventions of the Other Volume II,* trans. Kate Linker, particularly as concerns its being "*advanced* by an *advance* made to the other—and *maintaining* architecture, *now* architecture" (95; emphasis modified). See also "Why Peter Eisenman Writes Such Good Books," in *Psyche: Inventions of the Other Volume II,* trans. Sarah Whiting. Finally, the reader may consult Derrida, *Les Arts de l'espace: Écrits et interventions sur l'architecture,* ed. Ginette Michaud and Joanna Masó (Paris: La Différence, 2015).

32   Cf. Derrida, "How to Avoid Speaking," 171. Derrida famously remarks in the final interview before his death that "all the concepts that have helped me in my work, and notably that of the trace or of the spectral, were related to this 'surviving' as a structural and rigorously originary dimension" (Jacques Derrida, *Learning to Live Finally: The Last Interview,* trans. Pascale-Anne Brault and Michael Naas [New York: Palgrave Macmillan, 2007], 26). Derrida continues: "Everything I say—at least from "Pas" (in *Parages*) on—about survival as a complication of the opposition life/death proceeds in me from an unconditional affirmation of life" (51–52). See also "Living On: Borderlines," in *Parages,* trans. James Hulbert. Finally, the publication of Derrida's 1974–75 seminar *La Vie la mort,* currently being edited by Pascale-Anne Brault and Peggy Kamuf (and translated by Pascale-Anne Brault and Michael Naas), will provide the grounds for a fertile elaboration of these questions not only with respect to life and death but also concerning the concepts of "aiōn" and chaos in Nietzsche and Heidegger in footnote 35. Cf. *La Vie la mort: Séminaire,* Jacques Derrida Papers, University of California at Irvine Critical Theory Archives, MS-C01, Box 12, Folders 10–19.

for Derrida. The possibility of the Demiurge's death is not an external accident supervening upon the gift and promise but the very condition for their reception and inheritance. However, "this does not mean simply that only death or the dead can give. No, only a 'life' can give, but a life in which this economy of death presents itself and lets itself be exceeded. Neither death nor immortal life can ever give anything, only a singular *surviving* can give."[33] An immortal god, he writes in "A Time for Farewells," would foreclose any undreamt future for the gift and the promise, that is to say, would foreclose the future itself. In his inoperativity and finitude, by contrast, the Demiurge abandons his creation, goes on holiday, and says "adieu" to himself without return or "au-revoir," in an *abandonation* so that "we" may inherit the finite promise of the earth.[34]

---

33 Derrida, *Given Time,* 102.
34 Even the Hegelian god, whose departure from itself, its "adieu-à-soi" in its kenosis through Christ, would be insufficiently radical. In the dialectics through which God returns to itself, in its absolute, infinite presence, "the *parousia* of God would . . . forbid this other present which is also the gift to the other, the offering, the future of a promise or of a donation." We can thus see how the Demiurge's powerlessness intersects with the possibility of the promise. Unlike the infinite Christian God, whose promise is keepable, the Demiurge's is unkeepable because of his very finitude. See Jacques Derrida, "Preface by Jacques Derrida: A Time for Farewells: Heidegger (read by) Hegel (read by) Malabou," in Catherine Malabou, *The Future of Hegel: Plasticity, Temporality and Dialectic,* trans. Joseph D. Cohen (London: Routledge, 2005),

As that which makes the gift possible by resisting it, *khōra* "itself" likewise promises nothing. "Before the gift, before the promise, before the promised Land [*Terre promise*], [*khōra*] is a gaping opening that is not a void or a nothing but that which, because of this indeterminacy, can become a universal point of reference."[35] Important ethical, political, juridical, and

---

xli–xlii. See also Derrida's reference to this debate with Catherine Malabou in Jacques Derrida and Maurizio Ferraris, *A Taste for the Secret* (London: Polity, 2001), 84.

35 Derrida, "Questions à Jacques Derrida," 208. While Derrida warns against hastily "bringing this chasm named *khōra* close to that chaos which also opens the yawning gulf of the abyss" (Derrida, "Khōra," 103), he also suggests that the "ontological-encyclopaedic" conclusion of the *Timaeus* would consist in covering over the "open chasm" or the "gaping mouth" between philosophical oppositions and their wholly other opened up by *khōra* (cf. ibid., 104). It would be necessary, if we had the time, to enter into relation Derrida's readings of Heidegger on *khaos, khaine,* and *khōra* with Nietzsche and Heidegger's (and, of course, Deleuze's) readings of the notion of *aiōn* and the eternal return in Heraclitus. As Derrida explains in "We Other Greeks," "The 'one differing from itself,' the *hen diapheron heautôi* of Heraclitus—that, perhaps, is the Greek heritage to which I am the most faithfully amenable and the one that I try to 'think' in its affinity—which is surprising, I concede, and at first glance so improbable with a certain interpretation of the uninterpretable *khôra*" (Derrida, "We Other Greeks," 36). Cf. also "Différance," 22, where the trace suggested by this Heraclitean fragment is thought of as "older" than the Heideggerian ontological difference.

As Heidegger writes in *Introduction to Metaphysics, khōra* designates a notion of place [*Ort*] for the Greeks anterior to the notion of space as extension (Martin Heidegger, *Introduction to Metaphysics,*

indeed ecological consequences follow from such an account. Not only does Derrida identify *khōra* as the

---

trans. Gregory Fried and Richard Polt [New Haven: Yale University Press, 2000], 69). In determining being as idea, however, Platonic philosophy would have "prepared" the metaphysical notion of space by transfiguring *khōra* into extension (ibid., 70; cf. also Derrida, "Khōra," 147–48n2). Derrida, however, finds this notion of *khōra* as "preparing" [*vorbereitet*] "the Cartesian space, the *extensio* of the *res extensa*," troubling, problematic, reductive, and anachronistic, as all discourses on *khōra* must nonetheless be (cf. ibid., 109; cf. also "How to Avoid Speaking," 187). Seventeen years later, in *What Is Called Thinking?* and without mentioning the *Timaeus* directly, Heidegger recognizes that while Plato's notions of *khōra* or the *khorismos* meant a difference in place between being and beings, the difference itself would have received insufficient attention in Plato's work (Martin Heidegger, *What Is Called Thinking?*, trans. J. Glenn Gray [New York: HarperCollins, 2004], 227). For Heidegger, Derrida explains, Plato would thus have missed this wholly other site of being, or the site of the wholly other. Cf. Derrida, "Khōra," 104, 148n5, and "How to Avoid Speaking," 187. In *Memoires for Paul de Man,* however, the final sections of *What Is Called Thinking?* on *khōra,* the disjunction of the site and difference come to represent what in Heidegger's thought for Derrida exceeds the former's usual emphases on the proper, gathering, and jointure towards a thinking of the gift that intersects with that of the promise (Jacques Derrida, *Memoires for Paul de Man: Revised Edition,* trans. Cecile Lindsay et al. [New York: Columbia University Press, 1989], 146–47). Derrida also gives a thorough reading of the question of the gift in *What Is Called Thinking?* in the unpublished eighth session of *Given Time*.

Derrida goes on in "Khōra" to cite Heidegger's *Nietzsche* lectures with respect to chaos in Nietzsche preventing a "humanization" of being as a whole, including an overly anthropomorphic reading of the Demiurge ("Khōra," 148n4). On the subject of this groundless ground of his famous notion of democracy-to-come in *Rogues*, we are interpellated through it to

---

disjunction as the possibility of justice, Derrida refers elsewhere to Nietzsche's Dionysian reading of Hamlet. "It is against the background of this disaster, it is only in the gaping and chaotic, howling and famished opening, it is out of the bottomless bottom of this open mouth, from the cry of this *khaein* that the call of justice resonates" (Jacques Derrida, "The Time Is Out of Joint," in *Deconstruction Is/in America: A New Sense of the Political,* ed. Anselm Haverkamp, trans. Peggy Kamuf [New York: New York University Press, 1995], 36–37). The forthcoming publication of Derrida's *La Vie la mort* seminar, particularly its second part on Heidegger's *Nietzsche* lectures, will provide important opportunities to sharpen these arguments. Heidegger identifies what he sees as two perhaps opposed fragments in Nietzsche: the first from the notes of the *Will to Power,* XII number 112, in which Nietzsche writes, "Our whole world is the *ashes* of countless *living* creatures: and even if the animate seems so miniscule in comparison to the whole, it is nonetheless the case that *everything* has already been transposed into life—and so it goes" (Martin Heidegger, *Nietzsche, Volume II: The Eternal Recurrence of the Same,* trans. David Farrell Krell [San Francisco: Harper San Francisco, 1991], 84); the next in *The Gay Science, With a Prelude in German Rhymes and an Appendix of Songs* (Cambridge: Cambridge University Press, 2001), 110: "let us beware of saying that death is opposed to life. The living is only a form of what is dead, and a very rare form." (See also these fragments in *Cinders* cited after references to Baudelaire's *La Fausse monnaie* and Mauss's *Essai sur le don* discussed in *Given Time,* followed by an entering into relation of the questions of the gift and cinders: *Cinders,* 43; 49–51.) What Nietzsche seeks in thinking this unity of the living and the dead, the totality of the world as chaos and becoming, is to "dehumanize and de-deify being as a whole" (Heidegger, *Nietzsche, Volume II,* 94). As Heidegger puts it, however, "viewed as a whole, Nietzsche's meditations

radically rethink the condition of the social bond once the social is no longer limited to the human, the liv-

---

on space and time are quite meagre" (ibid., 90). The temporalization of the eternal return remains bound to a metaphysical, vulgar, and indeed human characterization of time. For Heidegger, any thought concerning beings as a whole must be related to the human thinking beings as a whole, and this is true of the Eternal Return, ultimately a thoroughly humanized temporality. As Derrida writes, Nietzsche's concept of *chaos* will determine whether, for Heidegger, the latter thinks of time metaphysically or in a humanized sense, or as something else. In fact, Derrida suggests, the entire problematic of Heidegger's reading of Nietzsche may hinge on this point. Heidegger reads Nietzsche's adaptation of Heraclitus's *Aiōn* in terms of totality and of the authority of the present in its eternity and infinity. When Heidegger summarizes Nietzsche's thought as the collective character of the world as chaos, he interprets chaos as the totality of beings. For Derrida, however, this rests on an implicit interpretive gesture in Heidegger; when Nietzsche uses the word *Being,* Heidegger, "in such a crude manner it's a little laughable," substitutes "the totality of beings," which he then uses to define chaos (Derrida, *La Vie la mort,* session 9, page 14). However, Derrida writes, this does not take into account anything that Nietzsche says about chaos as a chain, as a yawning gap, everything that should prevent chaos from becoming a thought of totalization. Cf. also Derrida's own reservations before Margel's adoption of the translation of *aiōn* by "omni-temporality," a term more commonly reserved to Husserl's Living Present. Cf. Jacques Derrida, *Edmund Husserl's Origin of Geometry: An Introduction,* trans. John P. Leavey Jr. (Lincoln: University of Nebraska Press, 1989), 148–49. Deleuze notably also identifies the time of the death drive, the time out of joint, the time of *aiōn* and the eternal return as the third synthesis of time in *Difference and Repetition,* trans. Paul Patton (New York: Columbia University Press, 1994), and of *aiōn* as the empty form of time against the time of Chronos and the Living Present in *The Logic of*

ing, or indeed the organic.[36] The figures Derrida proposes as the site of this reimagined sociality—that of the *"avant-premier,"*[37] the desert in the desert, the desert island, or the *terre sans terre* suggested above are precisely those through which the promise of the earth must be heard in its intersection with what Derrida calls a messianism without messianism: an abyssal, chaotic, "desert-like messianism"[38] beyond any revelation, apocalyptic eschatology, or teleology: a universal structure of awaiting and saying "yes," "come" to the event, the future, the other, and justice.[39]

Sense, trans. Mark Lester (New York: Columbia University Press, 1990). Cf. also Margel's reference to Deleuze's reading of *aiōn* in *Le Tombeau du dieu artisan,* 101n36.

36 Cf. Jacques Derrida, *Rogues: Two Essays on Reason,* trans. Pascale-Anne Brault and Michael Naas (Stanford, Calif.: Stanford University Press, 2005), xiv–xv, 82.

37 "That which precedes the first" (Derrida, "Faith and Knowledge," 59).

38 Derrida, *Spectres of Marx,* 33.

39 Cf. Jacques Derrida, *Deconstruction in a Nutshell: A Conversation with Jacques Derrida,* ed. John Caputo (New York: Fordham University Press, 1997), 22–23: "This universal structure of the promise, of the expectation for the future, for the coming, and the fact that this expectation of the coming has to do with justice—that is what I call the messianic structure." For Derrida's readings of the *viens* [come], cf. Jacques Derrida, "On a Newly Arisen Apocalyptic Tone in Philosophy," in *Raising the Tone of Philosophy: Late Essays by Immanuel Kant, Transformative Critique by Jacques Derrida,* ed. Peter Fenves, trans. John P. Leavey Jr. (Baltimore: Johns Hopkins University Press, 1999). Derrida explicitly refers to his works on Blanchot and Levinas regarding the "come" (ibid., 162). For the former, see "Pa*ce* Not(*s*)" and "Living On: Borderlines," in *Parages*.

1. Perverformativity and the Promise of the Earth

The discussion of the promise and its performative pervertibility constitutes Derrida's own most frequent point of reference to *Advances*.[40] In "Marx & Sons," Derrida explains that thinking a messianism *without* messianism as a universal structure of existence must complicate both a theory of speech acts and a Husserlian/Heideggerian phenomenology of existence:

> The possibility of taking into account, *on the one hand,* a paradoxical experience of the performative of the promise (but also of the threat at the heart of the promise) that organizes *every* speech act, every other performative, and even every preverbal experience of the relation to the other; and, *on the other hand,* at the point of intersection with this threatening promise, the horizon of an awaiting [*at-*

For the latter, see "At This Very Moment in This Work Here I Am," in *Psyche: Inventions of the Other, Volume I,* trans. Ruben Berezdivin and Peggy Kamuf. On the subject of the "yes," see especially "Ulysses Gramophone," in *Acts of Literature,* trans. Tina Kendall, as well as "A Number of Yes," in *Psyche: Inventions of the Other, Volume II,* trans. Brian Holmes.

40 On the "perverformative," cf. *The Post Card,* 136. See also Derrida's "Performative Powerlessness—A Response to Simon Critchley," *Constellations* 7:4 (2000). Derrida's readings of the Austinian theory of speech acts date back to his famous 1971 lecture "Signature Event Context" in *Margins of Philosophy* and have given rise to numerous debates and refinements over the years. Cf. also the debate with John Searle in Jacques Derrida, *Limited Inc.,* trans. Elisabeth Weber (Evanston,: Northwestern University Press, 1988).

tente] that informs our relationship to time—to the event, to that which happens [*ce qui arrive*], to the one who arrives [*l'arrivant*], and to the other. Involved [with] this time, however, would be a waiting *without* waiting, a waiting whose horizon is, as it were, punctured by the event.[41]

Derrida argues that the promise is not one speech act among others but rather remains presupposed by any performative.[42] I have already promised, responded, and said "yes" to the other before even opening my mouth; the promise is thus a nonactive act, interrupting any will or goodwill through the passive decision of the other in me, before me.[43] The loss of self-mastery in this passive decision, however, opens the promise both to the best and to the worst, even to radical evil. Derrida thereby identifies an aporia or paradox at the heart of the promise; in order for a promise to be a promise, and for there to be a future, the promise must be unkeepable, intenable, excessive, indeed impossible. If a promise could be kept, it would merely come down to a programmatic calculation of the future, and would not constitute a promise worthy of the name. Furthermore, it must always be possible that a promise pervert itself into a curse or threat, that the remedy transform

---

41   Derrida, "Marx & Sons," 250–51.
42   Cf. Derrida, *Monolingualism of the Other,* 67.
43   Cf. ibid.; Derrida, *Memoires for Paul de Man,* 20; "How to Avoid Speaking," 151; "Questions à Jacques Derrida," 200. For more on the passive decision, see Jacques Derrida, *The Politics of Friendship,* trans. George Collins (London: Verso, 2005), 68.

itself into a poison (*pharmakon*), that the gift be a gift of death (*gift/Gift*).[44] As he writes in *Memoires for Paul de Man,* "this singular aporia, which divides the act . . . no one can master it . . . we are already committed before any active commitment on our part . . . we are trapped *in advance* . . . it is, if we can say this, 'older' . . . as a past which has never been present."[45]

It was mentioned earlier that what is promised or given through *khōra* and awaited through the messianic structure of experience necessitates a reimagining of the space of the ethico-politico-juridical. Importantly, this reimagining must exceed the religious topologies of the desert of revelations and the Promised Land [*Terre promise*]; the promise promises no utopia or salvation.[46] However, it does propose a certain tolerance or respect that would maintain an infinite distance regarding the singularity of the other in any

---

44 On the *pharmakon,* see "Plato's Pharmacy." Derrida notes in *A Taste for the Secret* that this entire text is "nothing more than an elaboration upon a remark in *Grammatology*" (Derrida and Ferraris, *A Taste for the Secret,* 46). Cf. *Of Grammatology,* 292.

45 Derrida, *Memoires for Paul de Man,* 95; emphasis modified.

46 As Derrida adds, however, "even if on the hither or the other side of any soteriology, this promise resembles the salvation addressed to the other, the other recognized as an entirely different other (the entirely other is entirely other where a knowledge or recognition does not suffice for it), the other recognized as mortal, finite, in a state of neglect, and deprived of any horizon of hope" (Derrida, *Monolingualism of the Other,* 68). See also Derrida's reflections on the safe, sound, holy, and sacred in "Faith and Knowledge" and *Advances.*

social bond or bind.[47] When Derrida writes "nous nous promettons" in *Advances,* we are to understand this both as a promising to one another and as a promising of ourselves, both fracturing the self-identity of any "I" or "we." Any subjectivity or intersubjectivity therein is always exceeded by the wholly other that can be anything whatsoever:

> The self (*soi-même*) has that relation to itself only *through* the other, through the promise (for the future, as trace of the future) made to the other as an absolute past, and thus *through* this absolute past, thanks to the other whose sur-vival—that is, whose mortality—always exceeded the 'we' of a common present.[48]

The promise contracts an infinite debt beyond duty and restitution, a fault before which all are originary guilty, and a corresponding *one must* [*il faut*] within which the French also lets be heard this failing or default. Ethical responsibility is inexorably bound to what links any *doing* to the *fault*.[49] The promise is thus both necessary and impossible,[50] and it is through understanding what links the question of what to *do* to this

---

47 This respect, Derrida writes, would still be *religio*, but as "*scruple or reticence, distance, dissociation, disjunction, coming from the threshold of all religion in the* link of repetition to itself, *the threshold of every social or communitarian link*" (Derrida, "Faith and Knowledge," 60).

48 Derrida, *Memoires for Paul de Man,* 66.

49 Cf. *Advances*

50 Cf. Derrida, "How to Avoid Speaking," 153.

originary default that we come to a radical rethinking of the question "What to do?" "What are we going to do, what must we do with the earth, and with the human earth?"[51] With the earth, Derrida adds below, that we so inadequately call "human." This is not only an ecological question, he adds elsewhere, "even if it remains on the horizon of what ecology *could* have as its most ambitious or most radical today."[52]

2. The Gift of Time: Advance without Advance

Recalling the *Given Time* seminar in *Memoires for Paul de Man,* Derrida expresses the aporetics of the promise and those of the gift as interdependent conditions of one another.[53] We have mentioned that Derrida reads the temporalization of the unkeepable promise in *Advances* as "anterior" to any transcendental, phenomenological, or ontological account of time, as it would be to any "simple speech act or simply the act or experience of an anthropological subject, an egological consciousness, the existence of a *Dasein,* etc."[54] The

51   "The Countertime of Philosophy, *Advances,* below.
52   Jacques Derrida, "Que Faire—de la question 'Que faire?'—?" in *Derrida pour les temps à venir,* ed. René Major (Paris: Stock, 2007), 49.
53   "No path is possible without the aporia of the gift, which does not occur without the aporia of the promise . . . there is no gift except on the aporetic condition that nothing is given that is *present* and that *presents* itself as such. The gift is only a promise and a promised memory" (Derrida, *Memoires for Paul de Man,* 147).
54   "Threatening Promise," *Advances,* below.

pre-chronological time before time of aneconomic expenditure, irreversible loss of energy, and pure consummation would be the "same" impossible as the
unkeepable promise and the absolute gift. It is not,
however, without relation to these economic temporalities, but rather allows these to function through
radically exceeding them. As he writes in "*Ousia* and
Grammē," "time is a name for this impossible possibility."[55]

In the *Given Time* seminar, Derrida recalls Heidegger's mention in *Being and Time* of the two transcendental idealisms having pushed what the latter calls
the vulgar concept of time the furthest, Kant and Husserl, which we can only schematically develop here.[56]
In his reading of Heidegger's *Kant and the Problem of
Metaphysics*, Derrida recalls Kant's description of experience or phenomenality in terms of finitude and
receptivity. Unlike God's *intuitus originarius*, which
spontaneously creates its objects, the finite being's *intuitus derivativus* only passively receives them.[57] As is
well known, space and time are the forms through
which the finite understanding receives its objects.

---

55 Jacques Derrida, "*Ousia* and *Grammē*: Note on a Note from
Being and Time," in *Margins of Philosophy*, 55.

56 Martin Heidegger, *Being and Time*, trans. John Macquar-
rie and Edward Robinson (New York: Harper Perennial, 2008),
501nxxx.

57 The reader will note, moreover, that Derrida explicitly distinguishes the receptivity of *khōra* from that of the Kantian *intuitus
derivativus* (cf. "Khōra," 110, and "How to Avoid Speaking," 173).

Derrida, however, identifies a relation between time and the gift through Kant's notion of transcendental imagination (*Einbildungskraft*) that, like time, is at the origin of pure sensible intuition. What is received as time is no present being. Rather, the "I think" of the transcendental subject is constituted through a pure auto-affection, a self-giving that gives, but gives nothing, and thereby receives nothing. "There is gift [*il y a don*]—time—of something that there is not or that there is without being-present, and naturally without any present-being—thus no one—giving what gives itself as time."[58]

Husserl's phenomenology of the consciousness of internal time likewise designates the Living Present as the source and guarantor of the phenomenological principle of principles: that what is given to intuition be treated as a source of knowledge in its givenness *as such*. But Derrida explicitly distinguishes phenomenological givenness or *Gegebenheit,* the originary *donating* intuition from his understanding of the gift and Heidegger's *es gibt*.[59] The gift cannot simply refer to the phenomenological passivity of intuition, since it is impossible for the gift to appear *as such,* or as the object of a subjective lived experience. The gift is rather

---

58   Jacques Derrida, *Séminaire: Donner le temps,* session 12, page 17.
59   Cf. Derrida and Marion, "On the Gift," 58. Derrida anticipates the debate with Marion with respect to phenomenological givenness in a footnote to *Given Time,* 50–52n10.

an excess over intuition and phenomenality.[60] Just as there is, Derrida explains, a gap—indeed, an infinite abyss—between the phenomenological appearing of a thing and its objective, worldly correlate, so is there with the time of internal consciousness and objective, worldly time. The Living Present itself organizes Husserl's philosophy of time, within which transcendental subjectivity structures its present experience through the retention of a past now and the protention of a future now on the basis of an originary, material impression of time. But the production of the present "now" produces no existent being, and is itself originarily passive and affected as an originary impression. Here again we have the same auto-affective structure of a giving-itself-to-be-received, or a self-giving the received [*se donner à recevoir, le se donner le reçu*]. "And in the auto-affection of this absolute phenomenological datum, absolutely indubitable, the same lets itself be affected by the other."[61] This other time exceeds and disjoins the circular auto-affection of the Living

---

60   As Derrida writes in *Given Time,* "The temporalization of time (memory, present, anticipation; retention, protention, imminence of the future, 'ecstases,' and so forth) always sets in motion the process of a destruction of the gift: through keeping, restitution, reproduction, the anticipatory expectation or apprehension that grasps or comprehends *in advance*" (Derrida, *Given Time,* 14; emphasis modified). See also in this text, "the problem of the gift has to do with its nature that is *excessive in advance*" (ibid., 38).

61   Derrida, *Séminaire: Donner le temps,* session 13, page 13.

Present; it issues from a past that has never been present.

Derrida's reading of Heidegger's "Anaximander's Saying" further illustrates the ethico-political implications of this excess. Even in *Given Time,* Derrida had mentioned this work of Heidegger's regarding the duty "to give what one does not have," having also expressed certain reservations before the notions of jointure [*Fug*], gathering [*Versammlung*], and those of the proper or propriation of the event [*Eigenes, Ereignis*] as early as "Différance."[62] Justice or *dikē* for Derrida ought not be understood, as it is by Heidegger, in terms of joining, accord, or harmony, but rather on the basis "incalculability of the gift and singularity of the aneconomic ex-position to others."[63] As the giving of what one does not have beyond debt and restitution, justice ought presuppose a disjointure and anachrony in being and time[64] in order to be rendered to the other, both in its absolute precedence and previousness and as the futurity and coming of the event.[65] As he notes in *Memoires for Paul de Man,* however,

---

62 Cf. Derrida, *Given Time,* 3n1, 159–61n28; "Différance," 26n26, 27. Cf. also Martin Heidegger, "Anaximander's Saying," in *Off the Beaten Track,* trans. Julian Young and Kenneth Haynes (Cambridge: Cambridge University Press, 2002).

63 Derrida, *Spectres of Marx,* 26–27.

64 Cf. ibid., 32. See also Derrida and Ferraris, *A Taste for the Secret,* 56.

65 Derrida, *Spectres of Marx,* 33. As Peggy Kamuf adds in a translator's note, *prévenance* "ordinarily has the sense of thoughtfulness,

Heidegger is not just a thinker of gathering, citing the latter's own reflections on *khōra* as the different spaces of being and beings, the disjunction of the site or *Ort,* and how the *es gibt* of time and space overflows the question of being in "Time and Being." Heidegger's *es gibt,* Derrida writes, calls as a promise.[66] It is inaccurate to say that being is, since it is not a thing, or that time is, since it is neither a being nor something temporal; we can only say "es gibt Sein und es gibt Zeit." The giving of this *es gibt* must thus be thought before any present-being, as indeed anterior to the question of being. The event of being, its *Ereignis* is itself inseparable from a movement of dis-propriation or *Enteignis,* and thus not unrelated to the expropriating aneconomy of the gift.[67] It still remains, however, that Heidegger wishes to think the giving of being and time with respect to what is most proper to them.[68] If the gift is another name for the impossible, however, ought it

consideration, kindness, but is here being taken also in the etymological sense of 'coming before'" (ibid., 226n28).

66   Derrida, *Memoires for Paul de Man,* 146–47. The published sections of *Given Time* signal the intent to develop a reading of "Time and Being" in its never-published second volume, to which the seminar notes give some tantalizing insights. Cf. Martin Heidegger, "Time and Being," in *On Time and Being,* trans. Joan Stambaugh (New York: Harper & Row, 1972). The seminar notes for the concluding fifteenth session of *Donner le temps* very schematically develop a seven-point reading of "Time and Being" over the span of two pages. Cf. Derrida, *Given Time,* 20n10.

67   Derrida, *Given Time,* 19.

68   Ibid., 22.

not designate an aneconomic ex-propriation without return? How might this impossibility thus be named, thought, desired, or known? And again, what to do with the question "What to do?"

3. Advancing to Advances

Deconstruction could be said to take place in *Advances* in the *gap* that separates the possible time of philosophy from the impossible time of pure expenditure, the gift, or the promise.[69] Any naming, thinking, knowing, or lived experience of the gift or promise would occur through a relation *without* relation to this impossible, across the gap, Derrida writes, that separates the gift from economy. In this gap, "a dimension opens up where *there is* gift—and even where *there is* period, for example time, where *it gives* being and time."[70] As Margel writes, that the Demiurge would be incapable of indefinitely representing the sensible world in the image of the intelligible ideas is to risk its becoming an illusion of the transcendental type.[71] Likewise, for Derrida, the gap between gift and economy itself resembles a transcendental illusion.[72] If Derrida suggests in *Given Time* that the structure of the gift ought to reactivate the Kantian distinctions between thinking and knowing, noumena and phenomena, since the gift

69 *Advances*
70 Derrida, *Given Time,* 10.
71 Cf. Margel, *Le Tombeau du dieu artisan,* 150.
72 Cf. Derrida, *Given Time,* 29.

cannot be known but can be thought, he adds in the discussion with Marion that thinking is perhaps not the right word.[73] The Kantian critical machinery cannot be dismissed, however, because at stake here are the very relations between the powerlessness and passivity of time on the one hand, and moral and practical reason on the other, the imminent urgency and actuality of the question of "what to do with the earth?" and "our" promising and commitment of "ourselves" to make it so that the earth or world live on.

It was mentioned earlier that the spacing of *khōra* ought imply a total reorganization of the space of the ethico-juridico-political, of the *oikos* of economy and ecology. If no politics or laws can be deduced or derived from the Demiurge's promise, and nothing can be "done" with it, it nonetheless gives us to dream this reorganization through the impossible.[74] Even if the gift or the promise are impossible, "we do not give up the dream of the pure gift, in the same way that we do not give up the idea of pure hospitality . . . We continue to desire, to dream *through* the impossible."[75] But this dreaming must not remain, Derrida writes, "a sort of adoring and faithful abdication."[76] Even if knowledge and thinking entail the destruction of the gift, just as the successful performative and voluntaristic activism entails the annulment of the promise,

---

73   Cf. Derrida and Marion, "On the Gift," 60.
74   Cf. Derrida, *Rogues,* xv.
75   Derrida and Marion, "On the Gift," 72.
76   Derrida, *Given Time,* 30.

it is necessary to urgently commit, engage, and *pledge* "ourselves."[77] This resulting performative commitment, however, might be said to transform the very thing it interprets. "'An interpretation that transforms what it interprets' is a definition of the performative as unorthodox with regard to speech act theory as it is with regard to the 11th Thesis on Feuerbach ('The philosophers have only *interpreted* the world in various ways; the point, however, is to *change* it')."[78] And if, "to be sure, nothing can be *done* [*faire*]" with the promise of the earth, it is because it entails an urgent and pressing re-elaboration of the question "what to do?" (*que faire?*). What to do with the question "what to do with the earth?"[79] But "we" do not inherit the Demiurge's promise of the world, the world of promise as finalized, completed, or self-identical; the condition of its inheritance vows it to disjunction, overflowing in advance the oppositions between theory and practice, speculative and practical reason, passively *interpreting* and actively *changing* the world.[80]

---

77   Cf. Derrida, *Spectres of Marx,* 37: "Differance, if it remains irreducible, irreducibly required by the spacing of any promise and by the future-to-come that comes to open it, does not mean only (as some people have too often believed and so naively) deferral, lateness, delay, postponement. In the incoercible differance the here-now unfurls."

78   Derrida adds the original German here: "*Die Philosophen haben die Welt nur verschieden interpretiert; es kömmt aber drauf an, sie zu verändern*" (ibid., 63).

79   "The Countertime of Philosophy," *Advances*

80   The publication of Derrida's 1975–76 seminar *Théorie et pra-*

The Demiurge's experience of the time before time is terrifying because it reveals his powerlessness to indefinitely represent the world he creates, thus vowing his creation to finitude and dissolution. In order to inherit the Demiurge's promise so that the world lives on, "we" must likewise experience this same powerlessness before the impossible time of the gift or *autre temps.* Like *khōra,* this other time can only be dreamt, and Derrida proposes transcendental imagination, as a third or middle term between or before the opposition of sensibility and understanding, passivity and activity, receptivity and spontaneity, theory and practice, "a certain thread tied between nonbeing (the beyond of being) and time," as the means to dream this *autre temps.*[81] "We" are able to dream the Demiurge's terrifying experience of powerlessness because "the

---

tique will allow for an important elaboration of these questions, not only a rethinking of the Kantian oppositions between speculative or theoretical reason and practical reason, but also a rereading of the stakes of Marx's 11th thesis on Feuerbach. Cf. Derrida, *Théorie et pratique: Cours de l'ENS-Ulm 1975–1976* (Paris: Galilée, 2017). See also below, where Derrida inquires upon the relation between the antinomies of pure reason and the aporias of the promise. "What time and what reason (speculative or practical) does a theory of the promise fall under? And first of all an experience of the promise, and of the unkeepable promise?" Cf. "The Countertime of Philosophy," *Advances,* as well as *Séminaire: Donner le temps,* session 13, pages 3–5.

81   Derrida, "Tense," 50. Derrida also refers here to John Llewelyn, *The Middle Voice of Ecological Conscience: A Chiasmatic Reading of Responsibility in the Neighbourhood of Levinas, Heidegger and*

power of imagination . . . finds in χώρα . . . at once its ultimate recourse and its ultimate limit, its condition of possibility and of impossibility, its possibility as impossibility, its power as un-power."[82]

Once imagination finds itself dislodged from any notion of power of production, it is no longer a question of *making* this other time come about [*advenir*], but *letting* it arrive,[83] a letting that would be irreducible to the metaphysical opposition of activity and passivity. This letting rather ought to be heard in the key of Heidegger's *Gelassenheit* or releasement, as the French *laisser* also means "to leave," notions concerning which the *Given Time* seminar develops so many beautiful pages.[84] "We" are originarily indebted beyond the possibility of any economic restitution to let [*laisser*] the earth live on, the earth the Demiurge has

---

Others (London: Palgrave Macmillan, 1991); cf. "Tense," 55. See also Jacques Derrida, *The Animal That Therefore I Am,* trans. David Wills (New York: Fordham University Press, 2008), 107–8.

82 Derrida, "Tense," 73.

83 As Derrida adds in a footnote, see also on this question "Economimesis," *Diacritics* 11:2 (1981): 6; "The Pit and the Pyramid: Introduction to Hegel's Semiology," in *Margins of Philosophy,* 77, 79; and "Theology of Translation," in *Eyes of the University: Right to Philosophy 2,* trans. Joseph Adamson (Stanford, Calif.: Stanford University Press, 2004), 64ff. Cf. Derrida, "Tense," 281n1.

84 Cf. the seventh session of the *Donner le temps* seminar for some of Derrida's most touching reflections on letting and remaining. For more on *Gelassenheit,* see "Number of Yes," 237–38, as well as Jacques Derrida, "Sauf le Nom," in *On the Name,* trans. John P. Leavey Jr., 73ff.

left [*laissé*] us, not out of abandonment but out of love itself, "that is, this infinite renunciation which somehow *surrenders to the impossible*."[85] "We" must thus dream anew this letting, indeed, live it beyond any present experience, as the condition of "our" "own" living-on, "ours" and the other's. *Advances*'s foreword to Plato, then, would not be the *Phaedo*'s learning to die, but learning to live on, finally.[86]

January, 2017

---

85   Derrida, "Sauf le Nom," 74.

86   Cf. Margel, *Le Tombeau du dieu artisan,* 57. My sincere thanks to all involved in the Derrida Seminars Translation Project for the invaluable lessons in the art of translating Derrida, to Peggy Kamuf and Dylan Nassr for their rigorous readings of and comments on the translation, to Drew Burk at Univocal for his editorial guidance, and to Serge Margel for his encouragement with this project. All remaining faults are, of course, my own.

Advances

The Forbearers

—Once again the *Timaeus,* of course, but a different *Timaeus,* a new Demiurge, I promise.

Running the risk—the beautiful risk—of thinking an anachronic earthquake: like an aftershock from the absolute prehistory of the world, nothing less. And for the earth of humans, we are still thinking the shifting of grounds that would follow an immemorial tremor, an architectonic trembling . . .

—What the hell! But Plato's *Timaeus* is seen as one of humanity's oldest books! We always reserve a special place for it in the Platonic oeuvre—even within the philosophical library. What is more, does it belong to the history of philosophy? of philosophy *as such*? Nothing is less clear. And this old book of humanity's, which also says the origin of the human, this book of pure archaeology is also a monument of the Humanities. Since its first appearance it is one of the most cited works in the world, undoubtedly among the most overburdened with scholarly writing. One feels it growing ever heavier, becoming buried under the superimposition of these commentaries. Is it still a book, this stele sinking into the earth to the despair of archaeologists? Is it a book among others, this all too heavy and quasi-"canonized" archive?

—Well, why not resist the temptation of saying already, before anything else, "canonized"?

—For more than one reason, this strange *Timaeus* would have once been just as popular, if one can say so of such an enigma, as the Bible. It was in its own way a kind of Bible before its time . . .

—From where, then, comes the temptation to associate them again?

—It wouldn't be the first time. This connection, we shall see, is not justified only because it is a question of the origin of the world in both cases, in short of what comes *before everything* [*avant tout*] (ante, abante), of the absolute *antecedent,* an ageless forbearer that would precede even the provenance, and perhaps the promise itself, and the alliance . . .

—You speak of it as of a race between ancestors. Ancestors before the age would have been engaged in a speed race, in a competition between pure speeds, without any other stakes, expenditures, or upping of the ante than speed itself. They would be, like us, more than one, we would be more than one at the origin of the world. There would thus be this competition between all instants and instances to know in advance *who* or *what* comes "before"—and who makes the advance, who lends or promises to whom, in order to attract or engage the other. There would be nothing at first but advances. One would exhaust oneself in counting the advances made: promises, debts, debtors, creditors, believers. Who to credit? Who to believe? Who settles the accounts? If I am counting correctly, three *"advances"* interfere *at the same time,* in the time of a competition between different subjects: a motive comes in first place [*prend de l'avance*] (chrono-kinetic sense), a lender agrees to an advance and indebts the other (economico-fiduciary sense), a seducer makes advances (strategic or rhetorical sense of an erotics). What does one do then, once again, when one advances *oneself* so?

—It's also to wager. Let's wager: that from now on we will no longer read the *Timaeus* "as before" but wholly otherwise. Almost in silence, right here, with the construction of this *Tomb* . . . at this moment, the landscape has just changed.

—But is there ever a natural landscape, especially for a discourse on the origin of the world?

—No, rather, what has just been disrupted would be the established scenery, the crux and the dénouement of a dramatic action. For Serge Margel's book describes

a silent dramaturgy *before* the first act of the world.
And, as a result, a new interpretation or performance—
let us understand this word as in the theater—lets us
decipher the traits of an unknown character, indeed
another person under the palimpsestuous mask of a
familiar actor. The Demiurge of the *Timaeus* was undoubtedly only a role, a "character," as one would
translate from English, a theatrical and barely mythical
persona. Perhaps he has henceforth become *someone,*
at the same time a *dramatist,* a *dramaturge*—both the
subject of a laboring (*ergon*) and an action (*drama*), the
producer of an event—and an actor in the drama. He
is *someone* who, as his name indicates (*demiourgos*),
labors, acts, produces, creates for the people, the pub-
lic, the universal, but also, following Margel's extraor-
dinary argument, an inactive, finite subject, powerless
and subjected to laws as contradictory as they are im-
placable, a central but also strangely passive subject.
Everything seems to happen through him, and yet everything happens to him. He suffers what happens to
him, namely our world, nothing less. . . .

—Would you dare see in him the subject of a Mystery
or a Passion?

1

The Ci-Devant God

—We will decidedly have to resist the Christian or more generally testamentary (paleo- or neotestamentary) slant of this discourse. We will ask Margel if he can, or wants to, help us there—or not. We will ask him if he thinks in short that the *Timaeus* must be read *before* any Christian revelation, and especially what this "before" could mean. When, after certain Fathers of the Church, Pascal proclaimed, "Plato, to dispose toward Christianity," he also made a certain "before" tremble.[1] And then at the center of the *Tomb. . .* , we find or invent (to invent is also to find) the promise, engagement, testament, inheritance, sacrifice, debt, and therefore duty; the *being-before* [*être avant*] is thus linked to the equally dreadful ambiguity of a being-indebted to what precedes it, a *being-before* or a *being-owing* [*être devant*]—indebted—to a *being-before before which it finds itself*: a mortal Demiurge, perhaps already dead, a *ci-devant Demiurge,* a coordinator of the world

---

1   Blaise Pascal, *Pensées,* trans. Roger Ariew (Indianapolis: Hackett Publishing Company, 2004), 161 (S505/L612).—Trans.

before the immortal gods, a singular Demiurge *owing himself* to the immortal gods *before* which the Demiurge appears, but a Demiurge *before* which we are in turn indebted inheritors, so many instances that precede one another *before* the origin of our world, even *before* time. More precisely, a time *before* the other, for everything happens, we will come to this, in a gap between two times. We do not know if this interval between two times belongs to time. If it still or already falls under what we calmly call time. We will never know if it institutes time itself or if, anteriorly [*auparavant*], its possibility would have pre-ceded time. Of what kind of speed would we still be speaking should it get ahead of [*devancer*] time? This absolute acceleration is what one must think beyond knowledge. "*One must*" recalls here, let us not forget, the promise and engagement of the debt.

—In any case the question "*Who* is the Demiurge?" would thus become inevitable, it would henceforth replace the question "*What* is a Demiurge?"

—Above all and before everything, or almost, in fact, *there is Demiurge* there [*il y a là Demiurge*].

—What would such a declaration mean? What is thus promised? Demiurge, proper or common name?

—Before even knowing what it could mean, or mean to *say* (perhaps nothing, who knows, we shall see, a

8

tomb can be empty and the book a cenotaph), we will ask ourselves what this phrase might mean to *do*. To promise, to promise oneself, is to do, to do through saying. One will ask oneself what effect the phrase attempts to produce or risks producing. One might wish to come closer, attracted, fascinated, curious: to finally see the hidden Demiurge of which everyone speaks so much and that *there is there* [*il y a là*]—and what's it like, a Demiurge, that goes there, who or what it looks like, how it behaves, what it does when it labors, how it speaks and thinks and calculates. One might also take fright and flee: "Oh, there, there is a Demiurge there! Let us leave quickly, it is both mythical and mystical, the demiurgic, secret and dangerous, moreover, it doesn't exist and it recalls dark conjurations . . ."

There is Demiurge there. *There* is still *here,* in this great work of Serge Margel's, *The Tomb of the Artisan God.* This sepulchre is *here-below.* One could compare it to those poems called *Tombeaux,* works destined according to a law of genre not to describe or analyze the existing tomb but to institute it by means of a speech act, to keep, honor, bless, sing a memory in promising it a verbal dwelling more sturdy than stone. One could say, of those like Mallarmé's *Tombeaux* ("*Calm block fallen down here from an occult disaster . . ." "The buried temple disgorges through its foul/ sepulchral . . . mouth*" . . .), that they are immortal or rather that they deserve immortality if precisely their *end* was not solely to *promise* immortalization, promising it to the dead re-

9

maining dead, to the dead remaining in the tomb from now on.[2] To the dead of this "symbolic death" of which speaks so forcefully the author of this book, of this entombment. Whose hidden title would be, then, dare I suggest it, *Tombeau for an Artisan God* before being *The Tomb of the Artisan God.* This title would perhaps better express the properly demiurgic truth of the book. Serge Margel would have thus both written and described a *Tombeau.* His book would be a *Tombeau,* like a great philosophical poem. And he will have taught us, in the same stroke, what is established in the promise of a tomb, and how, in raising a tomb, erecting it in his tome, signing it, one guards or keeps a promise. Not a promise among others, a promise in the world, but a world of promise, a *promise as the world,* the always to-come existence of our world as promise.

—There is Demiurge *there,* if I understand correctly, first of all the one *of which* Serge Margel speaks to us and toward which this book overflows itself. For such a Demiurge would be *there, over there,* always there rather than here. ("But . . . there is no *here,*" the Socrates of *Eupalinos* was saying a moment ago).[3] *Over there,*

---

2   Stéphane Mallarmé, "The Tomb of Edgar Allan Poe" and "The Tomb of Charles Baudelaire," in *Collected Poems and Other Verse,* trans. E. H. and A. M. Blackmore (Oxford: Oxford University Press, 2006), 70–71; translation slightly modified.—Trans

3   Paul Valéry, "Eupalinos, or The Architect," in *Dialogues,* trans. William MacCausland Stewart (New York: Pantheon Books, 1956),150.—Trans

before any reference points to him. His being-there would not be that of a living being nor of a dead one, it would not even assure us of a presence. Tomb there is, and Demiurge, but the latter will have done more than live or die, something more and altogether other, he would have survived. By dying, however. Neither living nor dead: *ci-devant*, surviving, but surviving *as* dying. Dying [*La mourance*] and survival [*survivance*] belong to one another because the being-toward-death of the Demiurge, in its temporality of incessant imminence, is inseparable from a promise. And it belongs to the structure of this promise to first of all promise its survival, to survive itself, to pass through death. A "symbolic death," as the author diagnoses it. The Demiurge would be, from the beginning, a sort of survivor, thus a dying being who writes the world in the instance of his death, his own or the world's.[4] He haunts a memory, but the memory of a promise. The last will of a testament opens the chance of the future.

—But is there *one* Demiurge? A single one? No, perhaps more than one. The one of which the book speaks

---

4   One imagines him ready to subscribe, at all times, to what signs Blanchot's last *autobiographical fiction* and to what thus *remains* [*demeure*] in the moment of signing, *in fine,* as a final resting place [*demeure*]: "All that remains is the feeling of lightness that is death itself or, to put it more precisely, the instant of my death henceforth always in abeyance." These are the last words of *L'Instant de ma mort* [Maurice Blanchot, *The Instant of My Death,* trans. Elizabeth Rottenberg (Stanford, Calif.: Stanford University Press, 2000), 11].

in an exemplarily scrupulous fashion in its impeccable fidelity to the Platonic heritage and to the immense body of literature this corpus has engendered, but also in an inventive, provocative, insolent fashion—without compare. The Demiurge Margel speaks of is first of all the character Plato puts on stage, if one can say so, in the *Timaeus*. And then there is another Demiurge, who only resembles the first, who is the author of a demiurgic book, Serge Margel, inventor of the *Tomb*. It is not the same but it is not an other. When we say demiurgic book, without clarification or context for now, it is to declare that we stand in admiration. But none too reassured.

—After having put forth [*avancé*] the expression "inventor of the *Tomb*," at least if it's not still unconsciously, "*avant la lettre*," why not tie it to the Invention of Jesus Christ, another dying god, or the Invention of the True Cross by Helen?—so many Inventions that consist in finally finding the dying one, in discovering a lost site or body? Why not evoke all the Entombments depicting the burial of Christ?

—Patience. Let's remain with the Demiurge that there is. A strange name indeed, "Demiurge." It generally evokes an entire imagery, we hurriedly attribute a doxography to it. Those who have not read the *Timaeus* generally see a sort of demigod in the Demiurge, not a hero but an architect, as is often said, an engineer or artisan, sometimes a munitions specialist or a pyrotechnician, or further still a satanic sorcerer's apprentice preparing a blow, indeed a blowing up, a blowout that can go badly (*must* go badly—as this book also shows, in its own way). In the shadows, the Demiurge prepares an artifact, deep in a workshop or a back room. He always stays in the back, behind, and thus before [*avant et devant*] everything. Calculation and magic, ratiocinating alchemy, dangerous alliance of technology and occultism, indeed spiritism. Then again, as for those who have read, or occasionally taught, the *Timaeus,* do they not content themselves just as often with such an abstract, schematic, and cold figure? At the origin of the world, or rather the order of our *cosmos,* before it, the Demiurge is especially not a creator God, some maintain, the Demiurge can only contemplate intelligible structures that have preceded him since forever, eternal paradigms. His gaze thus fixed on the model *before him in front of him,* this contemplator only has eyes for this model. With a draftsman's or sculptor's skill, however, he inscribes, he imprints directly upon the "site." Directly there on a support that is in no way substantial, in the impassive receptacle called *khōra,* he engraves, as if by hand, images or copies. But the artist-artisan has no more created the space within which this printer imprints images by means of "typography" than he has created or invented their models. Everything is *before* and *in front of* he who finds himself *before* [*devant*] his model, before what is to be done, before his judges and heirs: the immortal gods, the intelligible paradigms, the *khōra* and the representations he inscribes upon it—and us. The Demiurge is before [*devant*] these, already owing [*devant*] them everything, but also before and in front of us. This is what many philosophy professors incessantly recall, and they have good reasons to do so. The Demiurge has no proper life (he cannot therefore die), he has no proper body worthy of the name. It is only an instance and a situation. One should not even speak, as I have just done, of his eyes and his hand. Let us say, and again in a figurative sense, that he has a visual faculty and a manipulating ability, just what is needed to observe the paradigms before [*avant*] him and calculate their inscription upon a quasi medium without proper identity—and this will then be the sensible cosmos, our world.[5] But this double operation seems so secondary, so subordinate in its calculation, so programmed and constrained by so many obligations that the Demiurge at bottom often himself seems reduced to a formal function, indeed a fiction, barely formal, barely in-forming since the forms come before him. We are interested less in the Demiurge himself, in a sense, than with the operations of a calculating machine: neither one of the immortal gods nor a human living being. But before [*devant*] the former and before [*devant*] the latter. We recognize neither feeling, experience, or existence worthy of the name in this "laborer," "operator," or "technician," nor passion, life, or death. Barely a will (but this is where things are going to get complicated). The *Deus Artifex,* as was said in the Middle Ages, would be at bottom almost as impassive as the *khōra* when it receives the copies, representations, and imitations of the ideas from him. This is at least the imagery, the widespread opinion, sometimes the pedagogy that Serge Margel's book has forever disrupted.

—At the moment the Demiurge is defined as a "technician," I wonder if this book is not obliquely an essay on *technē*. Margel does not place the question of "technics" at the center of his analyses, if the word *technics* ever even occurs—I don't recall anymore. And yet, because the theme of time, the multiplicity of times, the anticipation and delay in the promise come to play a major role here, I would be tempted today to read *The Tomb* . . . together with Bernard Stiegler's *Technics and Time,*[6] two books that are of course so different, as distant and original as you will in so many respects, but two books that are just as rigorous, innovative, and audacious, two great texts on time. I believe them to be fundamentally concerned with the same thing, the same Cause, and that they both lead us back to a kind of Greek event, at the edge of the mythical, in a dramaturgy of temporality that links *doing* to the *fault,* the work, labor, or *technique* to *default,* performance to finitude. In both cases, it seems to me, a *performative* logic of the event inscribes lack in the operativity of the

---

5   Bernard Stiegler, *Technics and Time 1: The Fault of Epimetheus,* trans. Richard Beardsworth and George Collins (Stanford, Calif.: Stanford University Press, 1998).

performance. By that token, it inexorably develops the question of ethical responsibility. Ethical responsibility must take the promise into account, which never goes without faith, commitment, testimonial or testamentary trace, gift, sacrifice, infirmity, a certain "idiocy," gambling with life, mourning, monumental memory, sepulchre, etc. It inscribes ethical passion where a reflection upon technics until now risked seeing nothing but an instrumental neutrality and operational calculability. It's enough to say that the Heideggerian heritage would be at work in both books, visibly and invisibly, at once accepted and circumvented—or contested.

2

Eve and Inoperativity
One Time before the Other

—At this point, let me confide a feeling, just a feeling, as a reader. Then we'll let Serge Margel's book advance on its own, I promise. This book indeed expresses itself with as much force as clarity. It justifies and demonstrates its arguments in such a rigorous fashion that a foreword here seems more useless or improper than ever. Except perhaps if, before formulating a hypothesis barely worthy of the name and tiptoeing away, we managed to confess a kind of feeling. But, I must also admit, I have some difficulty defining the quality or modality of the admiration I'd nonetheless like to share with the future readers of this singular book.

I imagine these readers as astonished, first of all, as philosophers should be, it is said, especially when we are speaking to them of nothing less than the origin of the cosmos, gods and humans, life and death, tomb and inheritance, survival, gift and sacrifice, milk, blood, and sperm. And especially when we pose the question of the origin of the world *even before* it is possible to ask oneself "Why is there something rather than nothing?" (For everything happens here as if this question had no more sense, no more future, as if we had to go back even further before it, before the time it still seems to presuppose.) I also imagine them worried, these readers, reticent or seduced, depending on the case, with many soon wondering what just happened. What happened? What is being promised to us? What are *we* promising *ourselves*? In what way is this book an event? An event that seeks to make us think otherwise the eventness of what comes, all the while speaking to us of what might have come about at the origin of the world, just before it, of course, but only speaking of it through rereading one of humanity's very old books otherwise, not the Bible, no, this is a question that will not let us be, but a book anterior and undoubtedly foreign to every Bible, the Greek book on which we have no doubt written the most since there has been philosophy, to wit the *Timaeus*?

If I speak in the first place of the sensible thing, of a *feeling,* precisely, it is because what is at stake is a question of a certain experience of space and time. At stake are form and aesthetics, as Kant would have said. What is at stake is a question of knowing what measures up to the intersection of time and space, to wit, *rhythm*. The affect of my first reading indeed concerns, first of all, the rhythm of this book. At the moment it proclaims very novel things to us, perhaps novelty *itself,* and perhaps some bad news, it seems to me, with respect to the most archaic and cryptic heritage of our concepts of world, space, and time, this modest and violent, scholarly and provocative work is deployed in an unheard-of fashion. It advances with the very slow acceleration of a pace of which I know few examples, an almost immobile pace. After a meticulous, reserved, and patient dramatization that seems to give itself, as if on the eve of everything, the eternity of historical and philological knowledge, a dramatic turn of events comes about, of course. One is more or less convinced it has taken place, but one still wonders if this is really at the most resounding moment, around the end, and if everything had not already, *previously* [*auparavant*] been displaced, in an absolute eve, if the settings, decor, theater, space had not been changed, if the very place of the taking-place (for it is also a book on the place, *khōra*), if the thought of the event had not been submitted to an invisible and inaudible displacement between two acts, between the lines, here or there, silently or in the hushed voice of a parenthesis, indeed the whispering of an erudite note—and even right from the Introduction. For the Introduction hides nothing, does not suspend an expectation, it clearly states the stakes of the final thesis. But because this thesis remains to be demonstrated, is promised in short (and the promise is the other great theme of the book), we know nothing so long as the promise is not kept. And what is promised since the first page, and thus before everything, even before the first act, it seems to me, are not only the "paradoxical figures of the demiurge." It is not only the demonstration, through the "violence" of a fidelity to Plato's text, of an irrecusable "aporia." What the Introduction does not announce, for it does not say so, not as such—but what it perhaps promises in silence, is this not the aporia and paradox *within the very structure of a promise,* of the promise in general? Let us give this question some time to rest. Let us simply recall that *it is a matter* there, that the Demiurge *is a matter of,* if one can say so, a time of *inoperativity*. Time indebts itself to an other, so, one time owes itself to the other, and owes it the time it loses or gains. One time gains speed another time.[1]

—Time as the time of inoperativity, that is in fact perhaps this book's question. Its name indicates as much, the Demiurge would generally be someone who labors, works, operates, an artisan or artist, sometimes a "professional," a technician, a (manual or intellectual) practitioner. In Greek, this can designate a cobbler, baker, physician, or magistrate. But the singularity of the Platonic Demiurge according to Margel (we do not know of any other that *does this,* that is to say, at a given moment, *does nothing*), is a certain inoperativity, the fatal destitution that vows him to inaction, retirement, and "symbolic death" in his powerlessness to inscribe the principle of conservation into genesis. He does not know how to prevent the imminence of decomposition or annihilation. As if a death drive (an "internal death principle," as Margel puts it) were at work in his opus

---

1   "Un temps gagne de vitesse un autre temps." It is likely that Derrida means "Un temps gagne de vitesse *sur* un autre temps" here; one time gains speed *over* another time.—Trans.

and his corpus. And as if, at the very moment of the poietic production of the world as representation, an autoimmune work of mourning silently worked against itself, against the very principle of labor that ought make a Demiurge of every Demiurge, thus a producer.

So the Demiurge suffers from unproductivity. It belongs to his nature to tolerate this finitude, to *suffer it*. But he *suffers from it* as well, for he is sensitive in his own way, and he can only be so on the basis of a desire for perfection—both finite, then, and infinite. He cannot and does not want, he cannot will or does not want to be able to make what he should make, to wit, a *doubly representative* world. This duplicity of representation is without a doubt the most effective lever in Margel's argument. For it supposes two temporalities. The gap or disjunction between the two times (one time before the other) would be the origin of this dramaturgy at the origin of the world. To the *noetic* or properly *demiurgic* representation of the world (to wit, the one that calculates the motion of the planets, regulates the universe upon knowledge—and knowledge upon the idealities of concept and number) would correspond a *cosmic* time. To the *genetic* representation of the world would correspond a time that resists its idealization by cosmic time because it measures nothing else and does not measure up to anything other than an incalculable expenditure, an irreversible loss of energy. Now, with respect to this time of consummation or incineration, Margel says something very serious. And the entire book is there to demonstrate this. He

declares that this genetic time (against which the Demiurge at bottom can do nothing) is not second but
first. It would come *before everything and before every
other time*. But to designate the "before," ["*avant*"] the
"anteriority" ["*auparavant*"] of this precedence, Margel is bound to scare quotes. What would in fact be a
time before time, a prechronological time? An anach-
ronical time, an anachrony of time itself, a disjunction of time by time and in time, *as time*? It's this
one, in any case, this time of the loss, this time of the
waste of time, this time of "pure consummation" that
Margel defines, in scare quotes, as "preliminary" and
"anterior," not only "preliminary" to the order of the
sensible world but "anterior" to the planetary order.[2]
The scare quotes no doubt are necessary to designate
the nonchronological order, the a-chronical or anach-
ronical dis-order of a time before every other time, of
a third and first time before the two times. They are
also necessary, no doubt, where, for reasons we will
return to in a moment, Margel does not want to say,
speaking of this absolute eve, "a priori" or "originary,"
at least not in the manner in which a transcendental, phenomenological, or ontological discourse might
do so. The time he wishes to speak to us about, and
on the subject of which the question "What is time?"
becomes problematic in its very form, would not yet
be the time of Kant, nor that of Husserl, nor that of

---

2   Margel, *Le Tombeau du dieu artisan*, 54.

Heidegger. The temporalization of this promise would be even more "ancient."

—What the hell!

—And yet, this powerless finitude, this dyingness of the Demiurge, is not the devil nor evil, it is not the Fall, Sin, or the Passion. So, what is it? Read the book right away. And because a foreword must be elliptical, allow us to conclude by quickening the pace toward the promised hypothesis. Let us do so in two stages and according to two anachronies, two failings with respect to synchrony or, if you prefer, *two countertimes*.

3

The Countertime of Philosophy
(Prolegomena to a Theory of the Promise)

To think a promise of the Demiurge, that of never *willing* the annihilation of the world, there must be, within time, the time of an eve before time. Three conditions for this, in fact, at least three *at the same time,* and all come down to thinking the promise *before time* or in any case interpreting temporality on the basis of the promise and not the reverse:

A. First, to interpret the will as "promise." "Will" here would be the capacity to promise beyond a present power, to will even where one cannot, it would be an in-finite intention: "a kind of promise," Margel says, taking on this interpretation and justifying it precisely through the limit that time imposes upon willing, forcing it to suspend or defer its implementation:

> Such that the world thus produced will remain indissoluble, in its global form, *so long as* [my emphasis, J. D.] the demiurge in no way *wills* (μὴ ἐθέλοντος) the breaking of its bonds (41 *a*). "The realm of the world depends upon my willing (τῆς ἐμῆς βουλήσεως)," says the demiurge.

This willing, which *we will define* [my emphasis again, J. D.] below as a kind of promise, would in fact constitute a stronger and more powerful bond (μείζοντος ἔτι δεσμοῦ καὶ κυριωτέρου) than that by which the world was created on the day of its birth (41 *b*).[1]

B. Next, to see *goodwill* in this demiurgic willing. A promise should never be a threat. In contrast to the threat, in good "performative" logic, a promise supposes goodwill: one does not promise evil and the promise should never promise a curse. Unless it is perverted in its essential destination—this is the entire problem. Margel invites us to think demiurgic willing as goodwill, an originally good will, to wit promising. This is what one could call the absolute axiom, even when this goodwill pushes the Demiurge to sacrifice, to "symbolic death," to withdraw from the world in order to let it be, so that the subaltern gods he just produced (the heavenly bodies) might create a mortal race. This race, our own, will learn to die. It will practice sacrifice, *like the Demiurge,* and thus make of its own death a promise of immortality.

—This is the entirety of philosophy since the *Phaedo* and the *epimeleia tou tanathou*![2]

---

1   Margel, *Le Tombeau du dieu artisan,* 88.
2   "The exercise, care, or practice of death." Cf. Jacques Derrida, *Athens, Still Remains: The Photographs of Jean-François Bonhomme,* trans. Pascale-Anne Brault and Michael Naas (New York: Fordham University Press, 2010), 31.—Trans.

— C. An infinite promise remains unkeepable or untenable [*intenable*]. It thus divides willing, even goodwill, and intention.

—What Margel does not say, at least not directly or not as such, is that there is here an intrinsic aporia in the concept of the promise. It is as if a promise, in its structure, ought to remain inconceivable, if not unthinkable. The story of the Demiurge, in short, does nothing but illustrate this, for this aporia (which is also the chance of the promise and not only a negative threat that would paralyze it) is no doubt stronger than even a god. It would come before [*avant et devant*] god. Its antecedence works the promise through; it prevents, obstructs, *and* perhaps sets any discourse on the promise into motion. The promise must always be *at once, at the same time infinite and finite* in its very principle: *infinite* because it must be capable of carrying itself beyond any possible program, and because in promising what is calculable and certain one no longer promises; *finite* because in promising the infinite ad inifinitum one no longer promises anything presentable, and therefore one no longer promises. To be a promise, it *must be able to be* unkeepable and must thus be able *not to be* a promise (for an unkeepable promise is not promise). Conclusion: one can never *constatively* claim, no more than for the gift, *that there is or that there has been* a promise. One can never establish this by way of a determinant or theoretical judgment. One can only—performatively—

promise a consistent discourse on the promise. Is this not what Margel does, like the Demiurge? and like everyone else? Is this not what makes his book a demiurgic and quasi-self-referential act? Is this not what makes an irreducible anachrony out of any promise and any discourse on the promise?

—If the promise of the Demiurge is unkeepable, it is, let's put it this way, a *matter of time*. But "matter of time" does not mean that things will settle themselves, and that it suffices to wait. Because it is unkeepable for the Demiurge, Margel's interpretive commentary explains, the promise must be renewed by us, by a human race that inherits the (unkeepable) promise from an other and thereby takes responsibility for it. But by the same token, it seems to me, this second promise confirms the *unkeepable promise*. It confirms the inherited *promise* in renewing it, but it also unfortunately confirms that it is and remains, in its very structure, *unkeepable*. It is a matter here of a responsibility—taken in the name of an other, as always—of our responsibility as well as that of an other, of a human responsibility that in short takes on the survival of the cosmos, or our world, in any case. Is there a more "current" problem? More current, that is to say more present, more urgent, but also more pressing and more acute in a new form of the question "What to do?" What are we going to do, what must we do with the earth, and with the human earth?

To analyze what we could call a *testament without precedent,* we would have to try to think time beyond any philosophical concept of time, beyond a philosophical tradition that has nonetheless established itself, let's say since the *Phaedo, in view of* taking this inheritance of the unkeepable promise upon itself, that is to say within the horizon of sacrificial death, of a given, received, accepted death. This tradition would not only be the one "deconstructed" by Heidegger, insofar as it is dominated by a vulgar concept of time; it would still be the tradition at work in Husserlian phenomenology and even in Heidegger's existential analytic. This book's immense promise, the one that will no doubt carry it beyond itself in the future, is the ambition of thinking this time of the unkeepable promise, the time of an expenditure without possible restitution, what in truth never lets itself be returned.

Before clarifying this point, let us draw the reader's attention to the richness, meticulousness, and rigor, and also the strategy of all the analyses of temporality. The most decisive moments of this strategy, it seems to me, concern:

1. "the two concepts of time" (ch. 1, IIb);

2. the translation of *aiōn* as "omni-temporality" rather than "eternity"; this translation with a word that has up until now been reserved for a Husserlian concept is one of the *two* decisive *choices* made by Margel,[3] even if it is guided by Rémi Brague's

---

3   "The temporal form of intelligible content" is not in time but indefinitely iterable: "This attribute [iterability, the "indefinitely repeated form of a unity"] thus does not represent the *contrary*

29

invaluable works on the *Timaeus* and this debt is clearly and frequently recalled;[4]

3. the three *forms* of time (numerical, or rather *enumerable,* time, neither enumerated nor enumerating, *genetic,* and *mimetic*);[5]

4. the instant (*exaiphnes*) and its strange (*atopon*) nature, as the *Parmenides* puts it; maintaining itself in the interval between movement and immobility, an instant does not belong to time; in short, it precedes everything, it comes before time;[6]

5. the beginning in the beginning, the beginning before or after the beginning (πάλιν ἀρκτέον ἀπ᾽ ἀρχῆς, says the *Timaeus*); this pre-beginning does not come down, Margel notes, to the

---

of temporality but a specific *mode* of temporality; and this is why we have chosen to translate αἰών as *omni-temporality*" (Margel, *Le Tombeau du dieu artisan,* 104). One of the pivotal points of this argument, it seems, is found in the translation and interpretation of the famous passage of the *Timaeus* (37 *c–d*) when the idea of producing the "mobile image of omni-temporality" "comes to mind (δ᾽ἐπενόει)," in the Demiurge. Cf. 92.

   Another decisive choice, another appellation, exceeds its merely terminological appearance. To speak of the Demiurge's "symbolic death" is a strong interpretation. It leads far beyond the letter of any Platonic text. Plato, of course, never spoke of this death of the Demiurge, and a symbolic death is not simply a death, a death without phrase. Margel knows this well: "It is what we will below call the symbolic death of the demiurge through the effective annihilation of the world. But, before getting to this final point, as salutary as it is disastrous, of mimetic production . . ." (Margel, *Le Tombeau du dieu artisan,* 96)

4   Rémi Brague, *Du temps chez Platon et Aristote: Quatres études* (Paris: Presses Universitaires de France, 1982).

5   Margel, *Le Tombeau du dieu artisan*, 107.

6   Ibid., 113n46.

most originary and oldest but to the redefinition of the founding principle: it is thus indeed a question of thinking the before in the before, the abyss of antecedence, the absolute or immemorial anteriority of the principle of the promise;[7]

6. the process of the linearization of time that makes loss or the nonrestitution of the singular irreversible;[8]

7. the interpretation of the *khōra* as memory, "the remembering force of a representation," an interpretation the author himself deems "perilous," and rightly so.[9]

To think the time of an absolute loss, of an originary expenditure without possible restitution, would be to risk, with respect to Husserl and Heidegger's analyses of time, a double gesture, doubly audacious.

---

7   Ibid., 117.

8   Ibid., 127.

9   To say that he *is right* to deem it "perilous" (ibid., 140) is to suggest that he *is perhaps wrong* to thus go against what Plato says on this subject, where Plato remains enigmatic but also quite forceful, one could say irresistible. Plato insists on the necessity that the *khōra*, as receptacle, let everything erase itself within itself so that it can "receive" the imprints. In other words, it must *itself* be a nonmemory. It must not only not remember anything, but not "forget" anything, if forgetting still testifies to the failure of a "remembering force." *Khōra* does not even forget. Already the persistent definition of *khōra* as a force, a "mimetic force" (ibid., 141) or a "spacing force" (ibid., 140) can seem problematic. But this only makes so many beautiful pages on the *khōra* more dense and fruitful: *khōra*, linearization, and hospitality (ibid., 121–1–55); *khōra* and food (ibid., 121); "aporetic structure of the receptacle" (ibid., 123), *khōra*, loss, and singularity (ibid., 128); *khōra*, bastardization, spectre, and spacing (ibid., 136–39).

On the one hand, to show how this time of originary expenditure "would be irreducible to any genetic constitution of the phenomenon and any ontological project of *Dasein*."[10] It would be just as foreign to the egological horizon that structures a phenomenology of time (Husserl) as it would to the order or existential horizon of temporal ecstases (Heidegger).

But, on the other hand, and by the same token, it would allow us to account (precisely where restorative accounting and calculation would be impossible) for the reconstitution of this restorative horizon, for the "possibility of a purely restorative formal configuration, presupposed by any genetic or ontological constitution of temporality."[11]

---

10 Ibid., 156n4.

11 A certain footnote (ibid.) seems to bring to its most daring formulation the hypothesis according to which the Husserlian and Heideggerian analyses of temporality would ultimately still be inscribed *within philosophical time,* to wit within philosophy insofar as, since Plato, it tries to "restitute," and thus to keep the Demiurge's unkeepable promise within the sacrificial horizon of death we were speaking of a moment ago. One can imagine all the difficulties of such a hypothesis, one should say this hyperbole, especially if one formulates it as we believe we must here. But at the same time, since it is also a question of accounting for the possibility of phenomenology and the existential analytic, in respecting this possibility, the most provocative also seems very reasonable.

What we could put to the test with respect to this "philosophical time," an enormous task, are perhaps the limits of a translation: between the aporias promised here, beginning with those of the promise itself, and the antinomies of pure reason (the beginning within time and space, divisibility, freedom, causality of the world).

Is this not to suggest that the goal of the *time of philosophy* (from Plato to Heidegger inclusively), or, if you prefer, the philosophical experience and interpretation of time, would be to *compensate,* to think in order to compensate, to resist the originary expenditure of this other time, this time before time, and thereby to aim at a restitution of this expenditure? In view of this restitution, in view of the promise to be kept, the time of philosophy would be a *counter-time,* one hopelessly opposed to the time of originary expenditure or the absolute gift. Philosophical counter-time would have thus inopportunely [*à contretemps*] come about in order to resist this other countertime that will have been the absolute time of the unkeepable promise,

---

Concerning the antinomy of the "forbearers" we spoke of earlier, let us think of what Kant says of the "pair of parents" (*Elternpaar*), of generation, of the given (*datum*) and the givable (*dabile*). [Immanuel Kant, *Critique of Pure Reason,* trans. Paul Guyer and Allen W. Wood (Cambridge: Cambridge University Press, 1998), 522 (A 512/B 540)] in "The Regulative Principle of Pure Reason in regard to the Cosmological Ideas" [ibid., 520 (A 508/B 536)]. The same "translation" ought to take account of what Kant claims concerning the presuppositions of "common human understanding" (*des gemeinen Menschenverstandes*) in the coming about of antinomies [ibid., 118 (B xxxii)], but also of the "play of merely speculative reason" that would vanish "like the phantom images of a dream" (*wie Schattenbilder eines Traums*) as soon as it "came to be a matter of doing and acting" (*zum Tun und Handeln*) [ibid., 503 (A 475/B 503)] ("On the Interests of Reason in These Conflicts" [ibid., 496 (A 462/B 490)]). What time and what reason (speculative or practical) does a theory of the promise fall under? And first of all an experience of the promise, and of the unkeepable promise?

the unthinkable antecedence of this time before time of which the Demiurge would have had the dreadful experience. This very experience would thus be demiurgic: experience itself.

Is the analysis of this experience within the grasp of a philosophy *as such*? Would philosophy as such, if this syntagm has any sense, be *up to* thinking this countertime of the demiurgic promise? Of the act of faith, mourning, sacrifice, testament, the tomb to which this promise remains promised? But can a religion as such advance itself where philosophy gets caught up in the aporia? Unless both precisely begin, and advance themselves, only where they are prevented from advancing.

4

Epinoia
The Countertime of Religion

—*The Tomb* . . . in short speaks of an old New Testament, of the "symbolic death" of a being that finds himself between the mortals we are and the immortal gods, before them and before us, owing himself to both. This book speaks of the sanctified sepulchre of this unique being, and of the gift and sacrifice of self, alliance, and promise.

—Yes. But, concerning Christ, dead silence. There isn't even an analogical evocation, comparative reference, preteritive allusion, nothing. We can give credit to the author, this is not mere inattentiveness. It is not the distraction of a reader who, disciplined in his internal analysis, would have shut himself up with Plato for a time, and even with only the *Timaeus,* refusing, precisely because of his historical and scholarly rigor, abhorring anachrony, to speak of something else and to jumble the contexts or orders of discourse. One must therefore look for other reasons to justify this silence. And recall that this silence is not an absolute silence on the Christian question, on a Christology in general, but on Christ and whatever possible analogy there may be between the story of the Demiurge and a neotestamentary revelation. For at least two signs come to break this absolute silence. These are two of the *Tomb's* "*parerga*," two hors d'oeuvres if you will, before the entombment and at the foot of the tomb: not *marginalia,* but an *epigraph* or *inscription* and a *footnote*[1] at the bottom of the page.

1. *First christological parergon: the epigraph.* It begins before the beginning and, like every epigraph, it amasses the infinite authority of what lays down the law. Here, the epigraph is borrowed from the *Confessions* of Saint Augustine—a great thinker of time, a common point of reference for, and so respected by, let us recall in passing, Husserl and Heidegger when they speak of time. Augustine, in short, ponders the possibility of the future. He especially reflects on the annunciation of the future by God, foresight, prediction, prophecy. But Augustine *is not saying something about time,* he does not say time, his utterance essentially neither states nor describes anything: he is speaking to God. Thereby addressing as much a request as a question to Him, turning toward him in the course of what is a prayer through and through, a praying meditation, he brings out clearly the paradox of a promise (a word Augustine nonetheless does not use here), he declares the aporia of a discourse on the future as promise,

---

1 English in the original.—Trans.

a discourse that does not simply predict or fore-see but makes come about. What seems so inconceivable, untenable [*intenable*] to him? That, essentially, keep-able or unkeepable [*tenable ou intenable*], the promise overflows *teaching,* which is also to say any theory, any *knowledge of what is,* any ontical, ontological, anthropological, or theological science. It is at this limit of knowledge, beyond knowledge, that a promise, and a prayer, is possible:

> In what way, then, do you, Ruler of all that you have created, reveal the future to the souls of men? You have revealed it to your prophets. But how do you reveal the future to us when, for us, the future does not exist? Is it that you only reveal present signs of things that are to come? For it is utterly impossible that things which do not exist should be revealed. The means by which you do this is far beyond our understanding. I have not the strength to comprehend this mystery, and by my own power I never shall. But in your strength I shall understand it, when you grant me the grace to see, sweet Light of the eyes of my soul.[2]

The difference between the (infinite) Christian God and the (finite) Demiurge is that the former's promise is keepable—or rather it is not unkeepable. But since, in order to be a promise, it must remain *keepable* without any assurance that it be *kept,* it must be able to

---

2   Saint Augustine, *Confessions,* trans. R. Pine-Coffin (London: Penguin Classics, 1961), 268.—Trans.

remain unkeepable, possibly unkeepable in order to remain what it will have been, to wit, a promise. But a merely keepable promise remains finite. The structure of the promise destabilizes the difference between the finite and the infinite, between a Demiurge and God the eternal Father. And in the same blow between the Demiurge and the immortal gods, which affects the founding distinction of the entire *Timaeus*.

2. *Second christological parergon: the note at the foot of the page*. It concerns the use of the verb *epinoien* (and not *noien*) to describe "what comes to mind," as Margel translates, and not the intelligible content of a noetic act. The *epinoia* (project, design, but also the thought that comes after the fact) marks the gap in the Demiurge's mind between pure knowledge and a moment of representative, reproductive and involuntary, "spontaneous" reflection. It is also the gap between "projection and its ideal object." In closely reading the few dense pages devoted to this, the reader can gauge the stakes and difficulty of this distinction—which seems to open up, if there is one, the proper space for the promise. Now, it is precisely in the course of this analysis that a long note situates a sort of possible mediation between this concept from the *Timaeus,* the *epinoia,* and what Margel himself calls a "christological context." Recalling a great debate between Eunomius of Cyzicus and Basil of Caesarea on the consubstantiality of Father and Son, the Unbegotten and the Begotten, Margel writes:

The ἐπι preposition in ἐπίνοια, still very *close* to the concept used by Plato, will have allowed, in a *christological context,* to engender a distinction that would assure a kind of *internal mediation,* as temporal as it is ontological, between the eidetic intelligence of the Father (the νοῦς) and the carnal attributes of the body of the Son.[3]

Here, then, is another node in the infinite entanglement of the relations between so many irreducibly distinct threads, *at least ten*: faith in general, the Christian faith, the Christian religion, theology—which Margel recalls must take into account at least "four categories of θεῖος in the *Timaeus*"[4]—Christian theology, theology in general, philosophy in general, Greek philosophy, Plato's philosophy, the *Timaeus,* etc.

How do we delineate a context, for example a "christological context," so long as we have not rigorously discerned among these threads? When will we have done so?

---

3   Margel, *Le Tombeau du dieu artisan,* 90n26. The words we permit ourselves to emphasize could lend their names to many obscure and serious problems.

4   Ibid., 162n8.

5

Threatening Promise
The Before-First Persons

—Once again, we were saying to the reader: open *The
Tomb* . . . without waiting. But if we had to pretend to
wait, we ourselves would once again put forth a *multiple hypothesis* (as one would say a *multi-socket adaptor*)
concerning the silence of the *Tomb* . . . with respect to
Christ, of the dead silence it imperturbably observes,
at least in its body, in the body of the work, if not in
its epigraphs or *parerga*.

First of all, a kind of hyperbole comes to affect all
the categories that could appear to serve the discourse's Christianization (re-Christianization or pre-
Christianization): the promise, symbolic death, gift,
sacrifice, tomb, testament, etc., the sanctuary, especially the monument dedicated to worship, of which
we have intentionally not yet spoken. It gathers together all holiness or sacredness (it is the chain that
runs through *heilig, holy,*[1] the sound and safe, the holy
[*saint*] and the indemnified, the immune, health, and

---

1   English in the original.—Trans.

salvation). It thus connotes the at least apparent re-
ligiosity of this demiurgy. All these sacrosanct categories generally presuppose a common ground: they
designate possibilities or events either coming about
to the world and *in the world* or *outside the world.* Here
the *agalma* Margel so often evokes, the sacred offering, the holy image, the sanctuary or sacrificial statue
is no longer this or that, this figure or this occurrence
in the world, or, moreover, *outside the world,* in view of
another world and in a movement of transcendence.
No, *agalma is the world,* the world itself. The world becomes something like the sacred archive of the promise, I don't dare say its Holy Ark. This changes all the
signs and displaces, indeed erases, all edges. The christological translation becomes, then, more than just a
risk. Not only because no sacrifice, gift, offering, sanc-
tification, promise, etc. can be determined *here, in*
the world; but because, if the illuminated vault of the
heavens, the demiurgic representation of the world,
is in itself an *agalma,* a monument commemorating
the immortal gods,[2] then the mobile image of omni-
temporality, the number we call time, would be but
mimetic derivations from the paradigmatic *agalma.* In
other words, the paradigm is already a sanctuary. It is
true that, if the world itself becomes a sanctuary or
"object of worship (*agalma*),"[3] and if the promise that
it *is* does not allow itself to be overflowed toward any

2   Margel, *Le Tombeau du dieu artisan,* 80.
3   Ibid., 55.

transcendence, the soul of the world itself escapes this immanentization. This is not a secondary difficulty of this discourse. The soul is "at once internal and external to the body of the world," it "would consequently be a being *outside* the world *in* the world."[4] And let us recall: when Pascal says, "Plato, to dispose toward Christianity,"[5] it certainly seems he is thinking first and foremost of the immortality of the soul.

Whatever the case with the immanence to itself of the world and the promise, if there is a religion, it would above all be *the Demiurge's,* that of the one who commits himself through an *infinite* promise, *necessary and unkeepable,*[6] that is to say, by giving his "word," one he can only bequeath us. We only know this word through interpreting and reaffirming its testament. This religion is not ours first and foremost, we can only inherit from it. This is not nothing, for from then on *we promise one another, we promise ourselves* [*nous nous promettons*] in promising him, *we promise one another, we promise ourselves* before him, before a "symbolic dead being," but this changes everything.

---

4 Ibid., 81.

5 Pascal, *Pensées*, 161 (S505/L612).—Trans

6 "The demiurge must keep his promises in a very specific time and place. He must commit his word very precisely where and when its noetico-practical taking-hold will have always already slipped away from him in time—in the time of the linear becoming of the genesis of the kinds. There would therefore be something both necessary and unkeepable [*intenable*] in this infinite promise . . ." (Margel, *Le Tombeau du dieu artisan,* 158).

43

How ought we understand the singular grammar of this utterance: *"nous nous promettons"*?

—What do we promise ourselves? Ourselves? To whom? what? us? the other? Would we be *promised* (like a promised thing, in some way: something promised, something owed), at once guardians and guarantors, inheritors or subjects of an unkeepable promise? Of an irresolvable debt? Both promised in the sanctuary and committed to watching over the site?

—The multiple hypothesis would thus yield at least possibilities. Hard to know if these will hold. Hard to know if they hold up, even implicitly, within this book, in what its literality seems to authorize. Perhaps we are being abusive, in opening these hypotheses at the threshold, before the book in its letter has even begun. The reader will judge. These possibilities undoubtedly lead beyond a re-Christianization of Plato or a demi-urgy of the New Testament, but they would give us to think precisely what they exceed. They would give this to us on the basis of the inoperativity of a gift, the gift of a promise or the promise of a gift that would perhaps come before any psychology, anthropology, ontology, and theology—in truth, any theory or *logos*. With everything it governs without limit, one can say that this chain of motifs (promise, gift, testament, survivor, tomb—site of memory as much as of forgetting, truth, sepulchre as *aletheia*) will never be reduced to a chain of philosophemes or theoremes—whether theological or scientific in general.

44

From this point on in this multiple hypothesis, the hypotheses of these *perhapses* are not mutually exclusive, they *perhaps* prop each other up.[7] "Perhaps" is not the very modality of the promise but the condition of possibility of any properly modalized promise, as of any hypothesis.

1. One can once again rely on the inexhaustible resources of an onto-theological teleo-eschatology: "Plato, to dispose toward Christianity" as to its truth—or the reverse, everything fulfilling itself in absolute Knowledge and the speculative Good Friday. Who better than Hegel read the truth of the Passion and the Testament within philosophy? Who better than him could claim to have deciphered therein the truth of a tomb, with the death of the mediator between the human and God?

2. Rather than confining oneself to the Platonico-Christian or philosophico-Christian pair, one could also seek out a common root, a universal paradigm of these two "examples" or specific determinations.

---

7   One knows the role the concept of propping or anaclisis (*Anlehnung*) plays in the Freudian theory of the drives. The first example of this is the sexual pleasure taken in the suckling of the breast. Margel also speaks of anaclisis in the beautiful pages he devotes to the "disappropriating process of lactation," as well as to the relation between the "lactation of milk-sperm and the cogitation of thoughts," between the "*milk-sperm* and the *ego cogito*" (ibid., 195–97).

This hypothesis can be developed in an anthology of religions or myths, an ethnology or an ethno-psychoanalysis of philosophy. It can remain in its raw state or become infinitely refined, beginning with rein-scribing the *Timaeus* into Plato's oeuvre and the Gospels into the corpus of the Abrahamic religions.

3. One can also, in a more synchronic and structural fashion, treat these two examples—examples among others—as a particularly rich and poignant material for whoever wants to teach, illustrate, or put to the test a general theory of the promise and its aporias. This book can also be read as an original propaedeutic to the great question "What is a promise?" If the theory of the promise was always before anything else, as is often the case, a theory of language acts, one would have to determine what is language or what takes the place of language in the demiurgy of the *Timaeus*: where is the Demiurge's "speech"? Is to bequeath an unkeepable promise to promise or threaten? For, as we know, a sound and classical theory of the promise cannot take a malevolent, malfeasant, or malefic promise into account. A promise belongs to the order of blessing. I can only promise something "good." I cannot promise the other to kill, rob, lie to, or damn him or her. This would be a threat and not a promise. Can one threaten with a promise? Promise a threatening gift? Perhaps. Perhaps this is the most profoundly worrisome question. For if this perversion were excluded from the beginning, if its exclusion were assured, there would be no promise that held up. Nor any threat.

4. One can also attempt to think what anachrony, as we have analyzed it here, admits into the three hypotheses: a dislocation of the present at the origin of the world, an interminable disjunction, a *constitutive disorder,* at once chance and threat, a condition of possibility that prevents what it conditions to comprehend, engage, determine, re(con)stitute itself so as to present itself without remainder. Infinite wound, infinitely and interminably inflicted upon everything that should be safe and sound, holy and saved (*hieros, hagios, hosios, sacer, sanctus, heilig, holy,*[8] sacred, saintly, unscathed, immune).[9] The promise we just spoke of is no longer a simple language act or simply the act or experience of an anthropological subject, an egological consciousness, the existence of a *Dasein,* etc. It is not in the world, for the world "is" (promised) within the promise, according to the promise. Not a promise from the human to God or from God to the human, nor of the human (as a being in the world) to itself, but a finite promise *of* the world, as world: it is up to "us" to make the world survive; and we cannot say this question is not urgently important today; it always is and always will have been, any time it can be a matter—or not—of giving oneself death, that is to say the end of the world; it is thus up to "us" to make what "we" inadequately call the human earth survive, an earth

---

8   English in the original—Trans.

9   Cf. E. Benveniste, *Le Vocabulaire des Institutions européenes,* vol. 2, (Paris: Éditions de Minuit, 1969), 179ff.

that "we" know is finite, that it can and must exhaust itself in an end. But "we" will have to change all these names, beginning with "ours," "we" know and sense this more than ever. "We" will have to "rename" everything, names that will come upon us more than we will choose them. We do not know what we promise (ourselves) when what we promise ourselves is "ourselves." Even if these are the same names we rename, of which we faithfully ensure the renown [*renommée*] and legacy, they will be other and will bear the trace of anachrony within themselves: "we" will no longer be (simply) gods nor humans; the world will no longer (simply) be neither the world (Christian concept) nor the (Greek) *cosmos*; life itself will no longer be what we thought it was, not always but more often than not until now: the simple contrary of death, as philosophers, biologists, and zoologists believe they can define it, nor even the being of beings in general, the "there is something rather than nothing."

As indeterminate as it remains, and so little unscathed, immune, and communal, a certain "we" resists. It can no longer be a case or a subject among others in a *theory of the promise,* neither in a theory nor in a theoretical response to the general and ontological question of the type "What is a promise?" or better "What is it to promise?" The theoretical and ontological discourse on the promise belongs to what it speaks of, it is overrun in advance by the performative of the promise that remains its element and implicitly or explicitly confers upon it its general form.

The thought of the promise or of promising thus presupposes, like every performative experience, what at least the grammar of a "first person" presupposes. It thus opens up, in the very "present" of this grammar, a nonsaturable future, the advance of a *to-come* that nothing could foreclose. But it also presupposes that this first person be plural, more than one, one and the other. Even when I promise *myself,* whether I am promising myself this or that or *I am promising myself to myself,* the other is already in place. One must make a place for the other because there is no place without it. What cannot be derived from this place is the "we" of one and the other, one as the other, even when the one guards itself from the other.

—If I understand you correctly, it would nonetheless be a question of a "we" without assured gathering, without intersubjectivity, without community or reciprocity, a strange dissymmetrical "we" anterior to every social bond. Strange . . .

—Strange, no doubt, but strange like the very condition of the social bond. The social bond requires such a "we," to wit, dispersion or distraction, the absolute interruption of absolutes, the *ab-solute* or *ab-solved* in a certain being-in-the-world that will have preceded everything. What comes before any promise, any promising, any "I promise," "you promise," "you (plural) promise," "they—masculine or feminine—promise" is "we promise ourselves" in promising to the other.

This "we" makes and undoes communities, indeed, it leaves no social bond at peace, no "intersubjectivity" or consensus. Its advance does not even let itself become enclosed by any horizon of expectation or of mutual understanding. In order for something to come and that the future of the promise remain open, the horizon itself, in the figure of its end, must be lacking.

6

Epilogue

—Even before the question "Why is there something rather than nothing?" we were saying "What then?" Not nothing—*khōra* is not nothing—but nothing that could be the object, theme, or content of some knowledge, judgment, or even a determining thinking ("this is that"). The future to-come of the promise, of what perhaps will be, or rather will come, can no longer *be*. It can no longer be a modification of the present—of the verb *to be*.

And this because of an ultimate paradox or final figure of the paradoxical or paradoxopoetic anachrony in general. Of course, to promise, one must *seriously know*, above all and before everything, what is promised. By whom and to whom—and what we mean to say and know when we say *we promise ourselves*. Knowledge and the serious, the self-presence of intentional consciousness as such, no doubt belong to the essence of promising. But if the promised in the promise (including the sense, subject, and object of the act of promising that form a part of the promised content) is absolutely known, determined, presentified, or presentable, if it even already has an adequate name, there is no longer any promise, there is only calculation, program, anticipation, providence, foresight, prognostic: everything will have already happened, *everything is beforehand [auparavant]*, repeated in advance. As what it is, to wit (as a certain Aristotle might have said) as what it will have been or what it will have been destined to be: τὸ τί ἦν εἶναι. We only conjugate some future-anterior tense here. Ruining the stakes, this antecedence of the *before* places the pro-position of the promise in danger—the promise it nevertheless opens up and puts to work. Anterior to the promise, anterior to the operational calculation of the laborer, it haunts the advance itself in a work of mourning that will have begun on the eve of everything. There would thus be two advances of the "before" ["*avant*"] beforehand [*auparavant*], an anticipation that sees what comes and a precipitation that no longer sees what comes. The precipitation we are speaking of here is not an empirical blindness or imprudence. Heterogeneous to calculation, it *lets come* or *makes come* on the condition, and this is the condition of the event, that it no longer sees what comes, on the condition of overflowing seeing or knowing, gaining speed over them precisely where they remain required. For there to be some promise, *it must* be the case that *nothing* overflow it or negate it in assuring it a guarantee, a provisional life insurance, mutual funds, social or communal security, the calculable probability of a prognostic: absolutely nothing on the horizon, neither thegod, the human, the world, nor being. For everything to depend on it and be inscribed within it *without knowing,* names must fail "us." *There must be names,* names must be in default, but this default will not be the negativity of a lack.[1] It will, moreover, owe nothing, it ought not, it ought not owe.

Indecipherable temple or mausoleum, tomb of the promise itself, risk of the cenotaph as wager: the risk run. For we do not know if these names that we lack are absent because buried beyond a given memory or are more distant than any given future. We must not know this so that a promise, if there ever is one, sees one day the light of day.

—So, if I understand correctly, for it to remain safe and sound, pure of any threat. But, we were saying, if this purity were assured, there would also no longer be any promise. Must not a promise, in order to

---

1 One would perhaps have to (we will do so elsewhere) cross this idea with Heidegger's when he interprets Hölderlin's ". . . *es fehlen heilige Nahmen*" [holy names are lacking] in a thought of salvation, the salutary or the saved (*heilen* and *Gruss*). This thought refers us to a default in the god, of course, but a default that is not a lack or a deficiency ("*Deshalb ist 'Gottes Fehl' auch kein Mangel*" [thereby "god's absence" is also not a deficiency]) (Martin Heidegger, "Homecoming/To Kindred Ones," in *Elucidations of Hölderlin's Poetry,* trans. Keith Hoeller [Amherst, Mass.: Humanity Books, 2000], 31, 45–46). But can we not risk saying, without or against Heidegger, that the salute [*salut*] to the other (*Gruss*) must suspend every assurance or every promise of salvation [*salut*] as what *saves,* in the safe, the salvation or salutary of health [*santé*] (*heilen, heilig*)?

"*remain* a promise, *risk*—this is what haunts it, what it continuously, incessantly risks, in an interminable imminence—perverting itself into a threat? Not only that it threatens to remain unkeepable but threatens to become threatening?

—In any case, the being-there of these names must remain what defaults the promise. And yet lack for nothing.

Absolute hypothesis, then: if the name of *khōra* still remains the first or the last word of the *Timaeus,* it is *perhaps* because it represents *one of the names* for *who or what* will have given place to all this, and will give place, of course, with the fore-seeing and capable hospitality of a "receptacle" (δεχόμενον), to wit, of *who or what* knows how to receive. But receiving and giving place without giving anything, impassively: beyond all natural generosity, without expenditure and without charge, without promising or promising itself anything whatsoever, only to receive and erase itself so as to give only in receiving.

—Only receiving instead of everything.

Jacques Derrida (1930–2004) was a French philosopher associated with the poststructuralist and postmodernist movements. He wrote more than ninety books, including *Of Grammatology, Writing and Difference,* and *Cinders* (Minnesota, 2014).

Philippe Lynes holds the Fulbright Canada Visiting Research Chair in Environmental Humanities at the University of California, Irvine, and is coeditor of *Eco-Deconstruction: Derrida and Environmental Philosophy.*